WITHDRAWAL

NEW DIRECTIONS FOR INSTITUTIONAL RESEARCH

Patrick T. Terenzini
The Pennsylvania State University
EDITOR-IN-CHIEF

Ellen Earle Chaffee
North Dakota University System
ASSOCIATE EDITOR

Using Qualitative Methods in Institutional Research

David M. Fetterman
Stanford University

EDITOR

Number 72, Winter 1991

JOSSEY-BASS INC., PUBLISHERS, San Francisco

Maxwell Macmillan International Publishing Group
New York • Oxford • Singapore • Sydney • Toronto

USING QUALITATIVE METHODS IN INSTITUTIONAL RESEARCH
David M. Fetterman (ed.)
New Directions for Institutional Research, no. 72
Volume XVIII, Number 4
Patrick T. Terenzini, Editor-in-Chief
Ellen Earle Chaffee, Associate Editor

January 23, 1991

LC 85-645339   ISSN 0271-0579   ISBN 1-55542-774-X

NEW DIRECTIONS FOR INSTITUTIONAL RESEARCH is part of The Jossey-Bass Adult and Higher Education Series and is published quarterly by Jossey-Bass Inc., Publishers, 350 Sansome Street, San Francisco, California 94104-1310 (publication number USPS 098-830). Second-class postage paid at San Francisco, California, and at additional mailing offices. POSTMASTER: Send address changes to New Directions for Institutional Research, Jossey-Bass Inc., Publishers, 350 Sansome Street, San Francisco, California 94104-1310.

SUBSCRIPTIONS for 1991 cost $45.00 for individuals and $60.00 for institutions, agencies, and libraries.

EDITORIAL CORRESPONDENCE should be sent to the Editor-in-Chief, Patrick T. Terenzini, Center for the Study of Higher Education, The Pennsylvania State University, 403 South Allen Street, Suite 104, University Park, Pennsylvania 16801-5202.

Photograph of the library by Michael Graves at San Juan Capistrano by Chad Slattery © 1984. All rights reserved.

Printed on acid-free paper in the United States of America.

THE ASSOCIATION FOR INSTITUTIONAL RESEARCH was created in 1966 to benefit, assist, and advance research leading to improved understanding, planning, and operation of institutions of higher education. Publication policy is set by its Publications Board.

For information about the Association for Institutional Research, write to the following address:

AIR Executive Office
314 Stone Building
Florida State University
Tallahassee, FL 32306-3038

(904) 644-4470

CONTENTS

EDITOR'S NOTES

The term *qualitative approach* is somewhat misleading. Although it provides a useful handle on a variety of approaches, no single monolithic qualitative approach exists. Many types of qualitative approaches are available, with different standards and criteria. Some types are in art, most are in science.

Qualitative Concepts and Techniques

The qualitative concepts and techniques discussed in these chapters—the emic (from the linguistic term *phonemic*) or insider's perspective, participant observation, interviews, and triangulation—represent only a handful of the available tools cross-cutting most qualitative approaches. Yet, together these few tools reinforce each other, improving both the quality and quantity of data in almost any research endeavor (see Eisner, 1988; Fetterman, 1989; Lincoln and Guba, 1985; Marshall and Rossman, 1989; Patton, 1980; Yin, 1984; for detailed descriptions of qualitative concepts and techniques).

The search for *the emic or insider's perspective* is fundamental to almost every qualitative approach. Qualitative researchers are interested in what people think and in why they think what they think. An individual's subjective perception of reality may or may not coincide with the stated institutional view of reality, but it has its own validity, and the individual will act according to that perception—with real consequences. The emic view helps the observer understand the values and motivations behind thought and behavior. This concept is so pervasive in qualitative research that it shapes almost every method used in the field.

Participant observation requires immersion in the daily life of the group studied. The researcher spends time observing the daily, weekly, monthly, and in some cases yearly cycles of a group's life and behavioral patterns. Research involves studying—and to some degree internalizing—the language, rituals, economies, and politics of a department or school. This process helps the researcher to understand more completely the people in that context and to ask relevant questions, grounded in the group's social experience. Qualitative researchers participate in the lives of the people that they study. They also step back and detach themselves from their surroundings in order to describe what they observe. This unique combination of insider's and outsider's perspectives creates a research view that is at once internally valid and externally consistent.

Interviews can take many forms, ranging from highly structured encounters to informal and conversational exchanges. Typically, questions are open-ended to allow the participants to formulate their own conceptions of appropriate responses. Once again, the aim is to elicit the insider's perspective or subjective conceptual framework. Ideally, the qualitative researcher begins with informal interviews to learn the appropriate questions to ask. Later, as the researcher gains a basic working knowledge of the social setting, the questions become more refined, focused, and structured. The practice of asking structured questions prematurely, before gaining adequate grounding in the social system, runs against the methodological grain of qualitative research. This kind of a priori approach is insensitive to the participants' perspective and typically results in systematic but useless information for program personnel and policymakers. However, if the structured questions are rooted in an understanding of the immediate social situation, then the structured interview is probably one of the most effective and efficient means of taking the pulse of a social context, including a college campus.

Triangulation is a form of testing the data. It involves comparing one source of data with another to test hypotheses and to probe more deeply into a group or culture, producing cross-validating evidence. There are many forms of triangulation and many names for it, but the general concept is basic to establishing validity in qualitative research. Like the behavior patterns that the researcher observes in the field over time, patterns of evidence exist that make a conclusion more or less convincing and compelling. Triangulation is one of many important tools used to document and describe what is going on in a community.

Fetterman (1988) presents discussions of the most common qualitative approaches in the field of educational evaluation. The authors in the present volume, *Using Qualitative Methods in Institutional Research,* use and combine many of these approaches, including ethnography, naturalistic inquiry, generic pragmatic (sociological) qualitative inquiry, and connoisseurship and criticism. For example, Tierney clearly represents an ethnographic approach; however, he also uses Patton's (1980) generic pragmatic (sociological) qualitative approach to crystallize his interviewing strategies and Lincoln and Guba's (1985) naturalistic inquiry to strengthen the trustworthiness of his data. I adapt ethnography to internal auditing, focusing on such traditional concepts and techniques as participant observation, informal interviews, and elicitation of the insider's perspective. Bunda draws on three different qualitative approaches in her work, including Lincoln and Guba's (1985) naturalistic inquiry, Eisner's (1988) connoisseurship and criticism, and Fetterman's (1989) ethnography. Louis and Turner rely on a case study approach. And Marshall, Lincoln, and Austin adopt a naturalistic inquiry approach. These combinations can improve an effort. However, the researcher would do well to study these approaches to determine which approach best suits the problem at hand, what specific concepts and techniques are most useful in tackling a specific problem, and what combination of approaches is most appropriate and effective.

Overview

In Chapter One, William G. Tierney focuses on the value of the interview as a tool with which the academic decision maker can gather information, develop hypotheses, and implement plans. This chapter provides a hands-on approach to the subject, focusing on such ethnographic basics as the structured interview, the informal interview, and the open-ended interview. Tierney explains what ethnographic interviewing is, how to do it, how to analyze the data, and how to write up the data. His chapter also highlights valuable concepts that guide interviewing, such as triangulation and trustworthiness, the emic view, confidentiality, and rapport. This chapter takes on additional significance as a lens through which to view and understand the methodological elements of subsequent chapters that rely extensively on qualitative methods.

Internal audit departments exist on almost every university campus. However, like qualitative approaches in institutional research, they are a neglected source of valuable information. In Chapter Two, I describe the general roles of internal auditing within a university setting, pointing out how the auditing function informs institutional management and thus takes on the characteristics of institutional research and evaluation. The many types of internal audits include fiscal, operational, electronic data processing, investigative, and management consulting. In addition, a new form of auditing is on the horizon: ethnographic auditing. Each approach relies on both quantitative and qualitative techniques. My discussion focuses on the qualitative approaches that ethnographers and internal auditors traditionally employ: participant observation, informal interviews, triangulation, and solicitation of the insider's point of view. Document review, interviews, and observation, for example, can together yield a full understanding of the unit being audited. Without this understanding, the researcher can miss important cues to organizational problems and potential solutions. This chapter demonstrates the utility of qualitative approaches in an area traditionally considered heavily quantitative and primarily financial. Ideally, this chapter will remind practicing institutional researchers that they already use some qualitative approaches, that they simply take for granted in their work.

Whereas I present an almost exotic area for many researchers—auditing—in an effort to distance the reader from the context and thus highlight specific qualitative concepts, Mary Anne Bunda, in Chapter Three, examines a familiar part of the institutional researcher's natural setting. Specifically, she explains how student portfolio construction is accomplished in the fine arts, where performance and qualitative judgment are fundamental elements. This case is particularly useful because it is intuitively reasonable to use qualitative approaches to evaluate qualitative areas such as the fine arts. Bunda includes such elements as the cognitive component, technique sample, breadth sample, and specialty recital. In addition, this chapter demonstrates how qualitative performance can be coded or quantified to inform curricular decision making. However, Bunda clearly explains how institutional researchers must work with the faculty to elicit their perceptions of reality as they attempt to translate and quantify elements of the curriculum.

In Chapter Four, Karen Seashore Louis and Caroline Sotello Viernes Turner turn our attention to graduate student socialization, which, like auditing, has been largely ignored in the literature. Louis and Turner demonstrate the value of using a case study approach to interpret rather than to measure the socialization process. They also highlight the use and value of interviews for institutional research, as students identify variables that have a significant impact on their educational programs. In addition, they reinforce the value of combining qualitative and quantitative approaches. Fundamental elements of their emerging theoretical framework, including structure, culture, and personal characteristics, provide useful insights into their three case studies of graduate education, including the socialization of minority women doctoral students. This chapter is particularly important because Louis and Turner demonstrate the impact of different methodologies (qualitative and quantitative) on the same policy issue.

Catherine Marshall, Yvonna S. Lincoln, and Ann E. Austin, in Chapter Five, adopt a case study approach, providing a descriptive account of Vanderbilt University's plan to study faculty quality-of-life issues. Verbatim quotations are used to convey the insider's perspective. The historical context, the values of participants, and the politics of the power brokers are discussed to convey a sense of the climate in which the evaluation plan was developed. The concepts and methods used to present their research findings are as important as the findings themselves in that they illustrate how qualitative approaches convey a rich and deeply textured portrait of a social situation. Marshall, Lincoln, and Austin also highlight the utility of combining qualitative and quantitative approaches, as the project that they describe uses surveys of faculty perceptions to provide an overview of faculty views, and individual and group interviews to supply more intimate and deeper insight into faculty work life.

Finally, in Chapter Six, I provide a broad view of the intellectual landscape. This chapter highlights qualitative reference material to guide researchers interested in pursuing the subject in greater depth and breadth. In addition, various professional associations that support a collegial network of qualitative researchers are listed. The list of resources is not meant to be definitive, only a good beginning.

Simply by highlighting the value of qualitative approaches in higher education, this volume makes an important contribution to the literature. But the volume makes an additional and more substantive contribution: It holds a wealth of qualitative information and enriches the institutional researcher's arsenal with a variety of new tools and new ways to use old tools. The chapters are designed as well to sensitize and expose colleagues to the rich diversity of the qualitative domain.

Clearly, some of the concepts and techniques discussed in this volume will challenge fundamental and long-held beliefs about data collection and analysis. This challenge is itself a useful contribution. Questioning of the basic tenets of any approach is invigorating and healthy. Whether or not this questioning stimulates readers to reexamine their research principles and practices, however, the volume forms a useful response to institutional researchers' interest in qualitative approaches that can facilitate the academic mission.

David M. Fetterman

Editor

References

Eisner, E. W. "Educational Connoisseurship and Criticism: Their Form and Functions in Educational Evaluation." In D. M. Fetterman (ed.), *Qualitative Approaches to Evaluation in Education: The Silent Scientific Revolution*. New York: Praeger, 1988.

Fetterman, D. M. (ed.). *Qualitative Approaches to Evaluation in Education: The Silent Scientific Revolution*. New York: Praeger, 1988.

Fetterman, D. M. *Ethnography: Step by Step*. Newbury Park, Calif.: Sage, 1989.

Lincoln, Y. S., and Guba, E. G. *Naturalistic Inquiry*. Newbury Park, Calif.: Sage, 1985.

Marshall, C., and Rossman, G. B. *Designing Qualitative Research*. Newbury Park, Calif.: Sage, 1989.

Patton, M. Q. *Qualitative Evaluation Methods*. Newbury Park, Calif.: Sage, 1980.

Yin, R. K. *Case Study Research: Design and Method*. Newbury Park, Calif.: Sage, 1984.

David M. Fetterman is administrator and professor of education at Stanford University, Stanford, California, and Sierra Nevada College, Incline Village, Nevada. He also is president of the American Anthropological Association's Council on Anthropology and Education.

Ethnographic interviews offer the academic decision maker an
alternative lens with which to gather information, to develop
hypotheses, and to implement plans.

Utilizing Ethnographic Interviews to Enhance Academic Decision Making

William G. Tierney

A new president arrives on campus and is concerned about the university's lack of community. A hazing incident in a residence hall leads an academic vice-president to inquire about what kinds of out-of-class experiences are taking place on campus. A dean of students wants to understand why 85 percent of the Native American students who enter the institution do not finish. Before she mounts another attempt, a new department chair wants to know why every major initiative geared toward changing the curriculum in her department over the past ten years has failed.

Each of these individuals needs information to make decisions, but the manner in which this information is gathered may not be best suited to traditional quantitative approaches such as survey instruments and analysis. Instead, the decision maker may need to utilize a different kind of lens to understand each of the above problems and to determine possible solutions. Interest is growing in the use of anthropological models and methods in the study of colleges and universities (Dill, 1982; Masland, 1985; Tierney, 1988). It is fair to say, however, that by the best of current research standards anthropological theory and methodology remain clouded in mystery for a large proportion of the higher education community.

In this chapter I discuss one component of anthropological research: the ethnographic interview. A discussion of the use and style of the ethnographic interview provides the reader with the essential tools needed to follow this approach. One does not need to be an anthropologist to make

The author acknowledges the helpful comments of James Fairweather and Robert Rhoads on an earlier draft of this chapter.

use of a qualitative instrument; at the same time, as with any research instrument, prior to using the ethnographic interview, a researcher needs to have a clear idea about the structure and guiding principles behind the research tool.

I begin with a definition of the ethnographic interview and discuss the rationale behind its use. I then delineate the processes used prior to, during, and after the interview. The chapter concludes with a discussion about how one may analyze the data and present the information so that it is useful for academic decision makers.

The Ethnographic Interview

Although anthropological research is a relatively new trend in the study of higher education, tools such as the ethnographic interview have been used by social scientists for over a century. Becker and Geer (1972, p. 133) provide a succinct definition of this kind of interview: "The interviewer explores many facets of the interviewee's concerns, treating subjects as they come up in conversation, pursuing interesting leads, allowing imagination and ingenuity full reign as the interviewer tries to develop new hypotheses and test them in the course of the interview."

Although examples of studies that have used ethnographic interviews in higher education research are not plentiful, they have increased dramatically over the last ten years. Chaffee and Tierney (1988) utilized interviews in case studies of academic decision making. Tierney (1989) called upon interviews extensively in an analysis of curricular decision making at seven institutions. By way of intensive interviews, Gumport (1988) studied how new disciplines formed at major universities. And Moffatt (1989) attempted an ethnography of college students by means of ethnographic interviews. Each of these works offers insight into how one conducts the interviews and what kinds of information can be garnered from the interactions involved. One finds that ethnographic interviews offer not only a different way of looking at a particular phenomenon but also a different way of thinking about the object under study (Tierney, 1985). That is, different research tools not only measure different data, but the questions that one develops and that arise from the data will also be different.

As Patton (1982, p. 161) notes, "The purpose of interviewing is to find out what is in and on someone else's mind. The purpose of open-ended interviewing is *not* to put things in someone's mind." The manner in which one collects these data, is, of course, not uniform across studies. In general, we can speak of three variations of ethnographic interviews: structured interviews, informal interviews, and open-ended interviews.

The *structured interview* operates within a standardized set of questions asked of the entire sample. As Fetterman (1989, p. 48) notes, structured interviews "are verbal approximations of a questionnaire with explicit research goals." The goal is to check for replicability of answers and variation across interviewees. Although the interviewer may deviate from the interview to follow-up on interesting points, the purpose remains to elicit responses to each of the set questions raised. This form is the least utilized format in anthropology but might be quite useful in institutional research.

The *informal interview* is a looser, more unstructured interview wherein the conversation may roam in any number of directions. Rather than search for replicable answers, the purpose is to let the interviewees offer their interpretations of reality without preconceived ideas developed by the interviewer.

Finally, the *open-ended interview* is perhaps the most utilized interview format in anthropology. Prior to beginning the set of interviews, the researcher develops a protocol of general questions that needs to be covered; however, the researcher is free to move in any direction that appears interesting and rich in data.

Regardless of the form used, interviews provide a holistic understanding of the culture of the unit under study, such as an academic institution as a whole or a specific department within the organization. As with any research tool the interview can help solve some research problems but not others. For example, if the researcher wants to understand how the organizational participants perceive the institutional mission or leadership, the ethnographic interview is an appropriate vehicle. Depending on the theoretical intent of the researcher and the purpose of the questioning, any of the three forms could be utilized. An open-ended question such as "Could you tell me what this place is about?" can provide a wealth of information about how participants perceive the institutional mission. Respondents at one public state college where I asked this question immediately responded about how the institution had a mission "to the working-class students of this state" (Chaffee and Tierney, 1988). Respondents at another state institution rarely spoke of anything connected with the mission or identity; instead, they talked about administrative deception and adversarial relationships.

However, if a researcher needs immediate answers to a specific question, then the ethnographic interview may not be the best tool to use. Needless to say, prior to any fieldwork researchers need to consider the assumptions behind their work and which tools are most appropriate to use. The ethnographic interview can provide researchers with a dynamic view of the world; all research problems, however, do not demand dynamic models.

Once researchers decide that the ethnographic interview is an appropriate tool, they need to have a clear idea about how to ensure that the research findings are trustworthy. A participant's perception of reality does not necessarily imply organizational "truth." Simply because a faculty member says that she perceives the mission of the college as service to working-class students does not mean that the college actually serves that clientele. An individual's response to an open-ended question also might relate to the immediate circumstances rather than to the overall picture of the organization. For example, if a department chair had a request for an additional faculty member turned down the day before the research interview, one might reasonably conclude that the disappointment clouded the chair's responses. For anthropological research in general, and for the interview in particular, the "trustworthiness" (Lincoln and Guba, 1985) of one's data is of paramount importance.

Consistent with the ethnographic tradition, the interviewer enters the field site without preconceived notions or hypotheses; rather, the researcher utilizes an inductive approach to the collection and analysis of data. The interviewer studies the organization as if it were an interconnected web of relationships and perceptions. The organization cannot be understood unless one looks at the structure and natural laws of that web as well as the participants' interpretations of the web. Organizational reality exists through the interactional processes of the participants. Hence, the ethnographic interview provides the researcher with critical data about participants' perceptions of the institution.

The assumption for the interviewer is that questions necessarily imply answers. In conducting ethnographic interviews, questions should be open-ended and nondirected as far as possible. For example, consider the following question asked of an academic vice-president (AVP): "What are the sources of tension between you and the faculty?" This question presupposes that tension exists between the AVP and the faculty. The respondent presumably could respond, "No tension exists." A more likely response, however, is for the AVP to outline areas of tension without first considering if the relationship with the faculty should be characterized as "tense." A more revealing question that an ethnographic interviewer might ask is, "How would you characterize your relationship with the faculty?" The question allows the respondent a wide range of responses: trustworthy, friendly, adversarial, tense, and the like. Thus, one key concern that the ethnographer wants to overcome is the presupposition or imposition of ideas or concepts by the kinds of questions asked of respondents.

One advantage of nondirective or open-ended questions is that they encourage spontaneity. The interviewer learns what the subjects regard as important. Langness and Frank (1981, p. 48) note, "Spontaneity enables you to learn how the informants conceptualize and think about their lives—the so-called 'emic' view that anthropologists have emphasized at least from the early 1900s." Instead of manipulating the research process to fit categories already outlined, the inquirer tries to understand the participants' worldviews. By using themselves as research instruments, interviewers can respond to concerns that arise during the course of the interview as well as adapt to the changing contexts of the interview. The interviewers' adaptability and spontaneity allow for the collection of data that otherwise would be lost.

Interview Procedures

The interview process involves a series of steps of which a researcher must be cognizant. In the following sections, I highlight and discuss these steps.

Setting Things Up. In many respects the procedures one follows to gain entrance to the research site are the critical building blocks on which all other research activity will stand—or fall. Once one decides on a research method and contact has been made so that entrance to the organization or unit is ensured, the task of choosing whom to interview begins. How the study is initiated is as important for an institutional researcher who works at the site to be studied as it is for the external consultant who sets foot on the campus or enters an academic unit for the first time.

How to arrange interviews, whom to interview, and where the interviews should be held are all important decisions that should be decided before discussion begins with the contact person. For example, an institutional research officer may attempt a study of faculty attitudes and need to gain the consent of department chairs. In this instance, each department chair serves as a contact person. Optimally, interviews are for forty-five minutes, with fifteen minutes in-between interviews in order to get to the next appointment and to provide time for taking short notes.

Careful selection of persons to interview is critical. If one is conducting a case study of a college or university, for example, one might cast this as a hypothetical example in order to use the third-person-singular frame of reference. Provide the contact persons with a detailed list of the kinds of people wanted for the interviews. For example, in a study about organizational culture at a college, I sent the contact person a cover letter and a list of the random sample of organizational roles that I wanted to interview. I included age-specific categories (junior and senior members), a wide spectrum of organizational roles (students, staff, faculty, and administrators), and beliefs (colleges boosters and skeptics). It is important to specify the kinds of people to be interviewed in order to avoid the pitfall of hearing one version of organizational reality, or of only interviewing the friends of the contact person.

In addition to defining the ultimate form that the project will take—a research report, a consulting document, a book, and so on—the contact person should be provided with a description of how informants' interviews will be used. Most important, issues of confidentiality and anonymity must be addressed. Before interviews begin, interviewees, the contact person, and perhaps the organizational president or head of the unit under study should have a clear understanding of the confidentiality of the interviewer's notes. If, for example, the report will be published and all individuals will be anonymous, but internally the report will be sent to the president of the college, then obviously the president may know who provided the information. Additional concerns might be whether individuals will be allowed to see the quotations attributed to them in the report, whether the interviewees can see the report when it is finished, and the extent of debriefing about how all the information will be used. Fieldwork should never begin with confusion about the nature of anonymity.

In order to help the interviewees feel more comfortable and at ease, and to make additional observations, the interviewer should meet individuals in their offices, or on their "turf." In that way interviewees do not have to walk any extra distance or feel watched as they talk in view of the administration. The disadvantage of interviewing individuals in their offices, however, is that interruptions are possible. The critical point to remember in the location for an interview is that a degree of privacy is needed, which entails a closed door or a space where other individuals will not overhear the conversation.

Similarly, the appropriate terms of address between the interviewer and the interviewee, as well as what the interviewer should wear to each interview, need to be considered. Degrees of formality and informality can play a critical role in what an informant is willing to divulge. Obviously, an interview with the chief executive officer of a major company who sits on a college's board of trustees warrants formal clothing, such as a tie and suit for a man. However, if a series of interviews is to be conducted with students who have dropped out of the institution and the interviewer wants the students to feel comfortable, the interviewer may want to look more informal and, again, not meet the students in the interviewer's office.

Some informants will expect to be referred to by their titles of rank, or honorific or professional titles; interviewees may be put off if the interviewer appears too casual. I also have conducted interviews where excessive formality leads to overly formal interviews that do not provide helpful data. The point is that no hard-and-fast rules exist, and that the interviewer ought to think about such matters as titles and clothing prior to arrival at the research site.

I have found that a mix of recording methods works best: tape recording, long written notes, short notes, and no notetaking at all during the interview but extensive notetaking afterwards. Tape recordings provide verbatim transcripts but are time-consuming and costly to transcribe. A tape recorder is also often an obtrusive instrument; microphones and tapes tend to make informants nervous. Notetaking does not provide the interviewer with verbatim transcripts, but it allows for observations beyond the informant's words. No notetaking denies the interviewer transcripts, but it can also help the interviewer focus on other sources of material, which can be noted after the interview: Cultural themes, spatial cues, how informants express opinions, body language used when speaking, and a host of other observations can all provide valuable clues about the organization. A mixture of transcription methods provides the interviewer with multiple tools for investigation.

Oftentimes, the reputation of the interviewer precedes him or her. "I had lunch with Joe," said one individual upon meeting me. "He told me you want me to tell you all the secrets about this place." On a project concerning Native American retention in higher education, another individual said, "I've heard that you worked at a tribal college, so you must have some understanding of the high schools on the reservation" (Tierney, in press). As with all the information provided in this section, there is no hard-and-fast rule about how one should respond. What is most important is that interviewers prepare themselves for a wide range of interviewees and responses. One cannot use the same techniques and methods from site to site, or person to person. If individuals lack the requisite training in interview techniques, then either trained interviewers should conduct the study or outside consultants should be brought in to instruct the staff.

Initiating the Interview. Upon arriving for the interview, the door is open and the secretary says, "Professor Smith is expecting you." The professor walks into the outer office dressed in a three-piece suit, sticks out his hand, and says, "Hello, I'm Dr. Smith. Please come in." Thus, prior to the interviewer saying anything, several cultural clues have been given. Titles, dress, and awareness of the interview provide the interviewer with a modicum of information with which to proceed. Always shake an individual's hand and let him or her direct the seating arrangement. Ensure that the door is shut. Again, the spatial dynamics of an office and how one uses space in an interview may provide additional insight about the interviewee that is helpful for the research. If one's topic concerns college advising, the spatial set-up of professors' offices might be quite helpful information; on the other hand, if the topic is strategic planning and the individual's ideas about the college's plan, then the spatial arrangements of the office may provide useless information. The point is that the interviewer must be cognizant of cultural cues in order to use them; whether one ultimately decides to use such cues is beside the point. The first order of business is to be aware of them.

Spradley (1979, p. 79) notes, "Ethnographic interviews always begin with a sense of uncertainty, a feeling of apprehension. This is true for both experienced ethnographers, and the beginner." The tempo and atmosphere for the ensuing session is in the interviewer's hands. Although interviewees may have received prior, written information about the interview, the interviewer should not assume that they have read it and should outline the project at the outset of each interview, providing information about the research, how long the interview will be, and why the individual has been selected for an interview. Essentially, the interviewer should try to make the individual feel comfortable. If one begins to ask questions immediately, it is entirely likely that the individual will not trust the interviewer. Intonation, affect, body language, and the like all communicate messages to the interviewee. The interviewer wants to impart friendliness, a desire to hear, and a respect for the individual's ideas and concerns.

As the interviewer talks, he or she should begin tape recording or transcribing. Again, it is important to make explicit how the data will be used. One might begin by saying, "I'm trying to understand the culture of the organization. I am not the president's confidant, and I will not talk with the president after this interview and relate what you said to me. In about (x months) I will have concluded my research and I will write a report. The individuals interviewed will be anonymous. It's conceivable that a quote or two of yours might be used in the report. If it's okay, I'd like to take notes as we talk. Before we begin, do you have any questions?"

The guidelines of the interview must be clearly established. If the individual says that he will only talk "off the record," the interview might be very valuable as background, validation data, but the information cannot be used in the final report. If the individual says that she will only talk if she can see the final report and a prior arrangement has been made with the president or contact person that the report will be confidential, then the interviewer cannot agree to send the individual the finished product. One alternative is to offer to tell the contact person that the interviewee wants a final copy, but it must be clear in the interviewee's mind that the interviewer will not send a copy without authorization.

It never ceases to amaze me how willing individuals are to be interviewed. Over the last decade of interviewing, less than 5 percent of my informants have refused to be interviewed or have even raised questions about the interview. Again, the point in the initial dialogue is to lay out the ground rules and make the informant comfortable with the person who is asking the questions. If the first five minutes of the meeting have been dominated by the interviewer, the rest of the meeting should be taken up with the interviewee talking and the interviewer guiding the conversation and listening.

Conducting the Interview. The way in which one begins an interview can range from an open-ended question such as "Tell me about this place," to a series of comments or semistructured questions such as "I'm interested in your experience here as a faculty member; I'm particularly interested in your perceptions of academic advising and how we might involve faculty more fully in the process." Both kinds of openings have strengths and weaknesses. The initial, single-unit question, commonly referred to as a "grand tour" question, allows the informant to give the interviewer a "tour" of the organization. The interview then proceeds from a large, open-ended question, and the interviewer can pick up on important aspects of the response as the interview unfolds. However, the entirely unfocused nature of the question can create confusion for the informant. Interviewees often approach interviews as if there are correct responses, or at least as if the questions will allow for yes-or-no responses. Consequently, a "grand tour" question may initially provoke hesitance in the respondent. The interviewer should assure the interviewee that there are no "correct" answers, and that the interviewer is genuinely concerned about how the interviewee perceives the unit or organization as a whole.

The more specific, semistructured question provides the interviewee with a focus for response. Extraneous information is avoided and specific points about "academic advising" can be ascertained. The problem with this type of question is that it may bias the data. The interviewer's question may convey an assumption that faculty are not involved in advising, and that more direct questions would not lead to pertinent data about advising.

Patton (1980, p. 207) has noted that there are basically six kinds of questions that may be asked on any topic: (1) *Experience* questions pertain to what a person has done: "If I saw you advising a student, what would I see you do?" The purpose of the question is to elicit descriptions of activities. (2) *Opinion* questions offer glimpses of the respondent's perceptions of a particular issue: "Why do you think minority students leave the university?" (3) *Feeling* questions are similar to opinion questions except that they are aimed toward understanding the emotional responses of individuals: "How do you feel about being the only Native American in a class." (4) *Knowledge* questions provide an understanding of what the individual comprehends about an issue. As opposed to an opinion about an issue, the purpose of the question is to elicit information on how much the interviewee knows about the topic: "If a student is at-risk at this university, what kinds of intervention strategies are available?" (5) *Sensory* questions probe the seeing, hearing, touching, tasting, and smelling aspects of the interviewee. "When you enter the learning resource center, what do you see?" "What does your adviser ask you when you go to see her?" Such questions elicit information about the stimuli surrounding the individual. And (6) *background* questions are the most common forms of inquiry. "How long have you been here?" "Have you taught at any other institutions where there is a significant population of minority students?" These kinds of questions are routine and help the interviewer contextualize the respondent's comments.

The quickest way to failure is to appear disinterested or bored. Conversely, if the interviewer can project empathy, interest, and rapport during the interview, he or she will have a greater chance to gain the confidence of the interviewee. It is important to remember that the interview is not a conversation that is equally shared between two people. The interviewer's judgments or thoughts about particular issues should not arise. For example, an institutional researcher who conducts ethnographic interviews at the same institution where he or she works may well have an opinion about a particular topic. Let me reiterate: The point of these interviews is *not* to validate the researcher's opinion; rather, the interviews should be designed to unearth data. If the interviewer is unable to divorce his or her own opinions from the topic under study, then someone else should conduct the interviews.

The interviewer should constantly want to probe what has been said. This can be done with a questioning look on the face, a quick movement of the hands, or a short phrase. Consider the following:

RESPONDENT: So basically, I'd say this is a friendly place to work. We work hard and get our work done, but it's friendly.
INTERVIEWER: Friendly?
RESPONDENT: Yeah, its like when I come here in the morning, everyone says hello to one another. We eat lunch together. Everybody knows everyone else. Even the president knows me. It's not like some big impersonal state university.

The interviewer's one-worded question—"Friendly?"—has provided a wealth of information. The interviewer gains an understanding of what is meant by the word "friendly" and of its reference point—another state institution. We gain extra information about other individuals such as the president, which can be cross-checked in future interviews. The response also allows for a natural flow of communication. If the interviewee stops and says nothing more, one logical next question might be, "What's the president like?"

The interviewer should observe three rules with regard to the interviewee's responses. First, all information is confidential. Even if the interviewee provides data that the interviewer knows is wrong because of something heard in another interview, it is not the place of the interviewer to intervene. It is also likely that respondents will ask the interviewer, "Well, you've been here for awhile now . . . what do you think of this place?" The response should express only the broadest generality: "The organization seems like a hard-working place" or "I have really enjoyed my visit and have learned a lot." This kind of response not only is ethical but also logically confirms for the interviewee that indeed all information is confidential. That is, an informant might think, "If the interviewer is willing to trade gossip about a previous interview, isn't it possible that he will also tell someone else what I said." Such thoughts discourage candor and open responses.

Second, if a respondent's answers are not understood, the interviewer should not act as if they are understood. One critical requirement of the ethnographic interview is the ability of the interviewer to speak the language of the informants (Conklin, 1968). If a respondent says, "The PTL used to be in a big airy room, but now they've moved it to Building Seven," the interviewer should probe for the meaning of the statement. A question such as, "The PTL? Building Seven?" can prompt useful information: "The part-timer's lounge. It used to be in the center of campus, but now they've moved it to Building Seven—way over in the far corner of campus. We call it Siberia over there. This new president doesn't care about you if you're not full-time faculty."

Third, although the interviewer should not interject opinions or ideas, it is important to express an opinion at particular times. Respondent comments that are racist, sexist, or homophobic and go unchallenged, for example, may lead the respondent to assume that the interviewer concurs with what is being said. The point is that although the interviewer does not want to get involved in a debate with the interviewee, the interviewer also should not come across as a passive object with no moral code or personality whatsoever. Far too often interviewers assume that to be objective, they must not project any appearance of personality. Humor, personal integrity, interest, and friendliness do not have to imply casualness or subjectivity; rather, each quality can help develop a working relationship with the informant in order to elicit information that is otherwise unavailable.

Indeed, one of the strengths of the ethnographic interview is that the interviewer is not a leaden object without personality. Although the interviewer wants to be neutral toward statements and data, a degree of rapport and empathy must develop between the respondent and interviewer. Patton (1980, p. 231) notes, "Rapport means that I respect the people being interviewed, so what they say is important because of who is saying it. I want to convey to them that their knowledge, experiences, attitudes, and feelings are important. Yet the content of what they say to me is not important. Rapport is built on the ability to convey empathy and understanding without judgment."

As the interview progresses, periodic summaries are useful where the interviewer summarizes a topic in order to ensure accuracy before continuing to another point. For example, one might say, "You've noted that minority students seem to avoid using the learning resource center in the Student Services Building. You've also said that those skill centers that are located in dorms seem to be utilized more frequently. Could you comment on that?" By summarizing one topic the interviewer allows the respondent to correct misunderstandings, to play back what has been said, and to move on to another topic.

Toward the end of the interview there is a need to both summarize and move toward conclusion. A summary statement might include, "I don't want to keep you much longer, but let me see if I can accurately summarize what you've said. . . . Are there things I have gotten wrong or left out? Is there something else I should have asked, that I didn't?" After the informant has made corrections, or provided additional insight, the interviewer can conclude with a word of thanks. "I appreciate the time you've taken to talk with me. I will be here for the rest of the week. If there's anything else that you think about that I should know, please contact me."

Postinterview Procedures

Immediately after an interview the interviewer should fill out a cover sheet. The cover sheet should have been developed prior to the interview, based on the interview protocol. The cover sheet should have space for basic background information for the interviewee, and space to record in outline fashion the central topics that were covered. These written cues will provide reminders to the interviewers, once they have returned to their offices, about what topics or themes were considered important immediately after the interaction.

If possible, a brief follow-up note to each interviewee is advised. Upon returning home I send everyone interviewed a simple note thanking them in writing for the time that they took out of their schedules to be interviewed. If a return visit will be held, I mention when I plan to return and that it is conceivable I will want to talk with them again. I also encourage them to keep in touch with me should they have any additional thoughts about the interviews that they would like to share with me.

Analyzing Data. After initial interviews have been concluded, it is essential that soon thereafter the interviewer review the notes and provide a written summary. This analysis should be done within twenty-four hours of each interview. When the interviewer finishes data collection, another systematic review should be done of the entire body of transcripts in order to probe for general themes and contradictions. All in all, the researcher should read the contents of the interview sheets at least four times: immediately after the interview, after all of the interviews have been concluded, at home prior to writing the report, and after the rough draft has been written. The point is to develop so thorough a familiarity with the notes that bits and pieces of cultural data are not overlooked. While one reviews the composite notes from the interviews, he or she will develop "cultural themes." Spradley (1980, p. 141) defines a cultural theme as "any principle recurrent in a number of domains, tacit or explicit, and serving as a relationship among subsystems of cultural meaning." Cultural meanings arise from the analysis of data. Return visits allow the researcher to test the trustworthiness of initial assumptions.

A primary concern for qualitative researchers is the trustworthiness of data. Indeed, the strength of qualitative research is the ability to provide "thick description" (Geertz, 1973) in order to understand the situation. Guba and Lincoln (1981, p. 150) write, "Portrayal should not only engender understanding in concerned audiences. It should also involve and move those who have never been to the site but who intuitively sense, through the report, that they could have been part of it." To ensure accuracy, however, one must guard against atypical informants, sources with low credibility, and interviewer misperceptions.

Atypical informants can be avoided by having a clear research design prior to entering the situation so that the interviewer is clear about who should be interviewed. As multiple interviews occur, information can be cross-checked. As contradictions in respondents' answers arise, such puzzles can be noted and interviewees can be asked about the inconsistencies. A fair amount of rapport and empathy with informants can also lessen the possibility of misinformation being given. The credibility of sources can be checked as the researcher discerns cultural themes and then reviews the multiple data sources for corroboration across informants. If the interviewer does not begin with preconceived notions about the research, then misperceptions will not be so frequent. In addition, constant rechecking with informants about what they said and reanalysis of data can provide checks for interviewer misperceptions during the interviews and afterward during the analysis phase.

Data analysis entails making sense of the data by discerning patterns in the interviews. Unlike statistical analysis, the point is not to generalize across contexts but rather to come to terms with specific situations. Fetterman (1989, p. 89) has provided helpful advice about how to cross-check one's findings: "Triangulation is basic in ethnographic research. It is at the heart of ethnographic validity, testing one source of information against another to strip away alternative explanations and prove a hypothesis." Data triangulation pertains to the use of a variety of data sources in a study, the use of several researchers, the use of multiple perspectives to interpret the data, the use of multiple methods, or various combinations of these four methods (Patton, 1980, p. 109).

Clearly, then, one way to triangulate ethnographic interviews is to conduct them in conjunction with other methodological tools such as observations or surveys. If, however, one uses strictly ethnographic interviews, then one should rely on the technique of constant comparison and contrast among informants and the data collected. The three forms of interviews, and the multiple devices used to collect data, form another way to triangulate data. Content analysis of the transcripts and probing of informants for their perceptions of the research findings also add to data trustworthiness.

Writing the Report. Obviously, the reports of institutional researchers will differ dramatically from academic studies. Moffatt (1989), for example, has written a three-hundred-page ethnography of college students that offers an in-depth understanding of the lives of undergraduates; an institutional research officer may attempt a less in-depth study of college students, and the text must be shorter and, if typical, offer implications for policy. One essential question for the institutional research officer, however, is the same as that pondered by the academic: How much description should be included? Patton (1980, p. 343) notes that "description and quotation are the essential ingredients of qualitative inquiry. Sufficient description and direct quotations should be included to allow the reader to enter into the situation and thoughts of the people represented in the report. Description should stop short, however, if becoming trivial and mundane. Again, the problem of focus."

The point is that the purpose of description is to highlight particular issues derived from the data. A good report offers enough description to enable the reader to agree with the analysis and to provide the reader with an understanding of how the author verified the data. For example, if one talks about the problem of retaining American Indian students in college, one might say, "Every student interviewed pointed out the problem of initial socialization on campus. One student, for example, commented, 'No one told me freshmen were supposed to arrive here early, and when I finally arrived, all of the classes were filled.' " Informant comments, such as the one cited above, aid the reader in understanding how the author arrived at the conclusion that "initial socialization" is a problem for minority students.

Conclusion

The ethnographic interview provides the researcher with information unavailable through questionnaires, statistical surveys, or predetermined question-answer formats where the interviewer tests hypotheses. In order to uncover the perceptions and attitudes of informants in an organization, the ethnographic interview is one tool available to the researcher. As with any research instrument, however, there are specific techniques that must be followed in order to use the tool correctly. Further, most research tools are not applied in isolation; participant observation, ethnohistorical research, surveys, and the like most often accompany the ethnographic interview. The methodological package can only strengthen the validity of one's findings.

I conclude with five categories of questions that institutional researchers should consider prior to using ethnographic interviews: (1) *Research focus:* What kinds of information does the researcher desire to gather from ethnographic interviews? In essence, what will the research protocol look like? (2) *Researcher bias:* Is the researcher so close to the topic that objectivity is impossible? Is the protocol built so that informants are able to develop their own conceptual categories and responses, or do the researcher's preconceived notions inherently bias the data toward a predetermined outcome? (3) *Interview design:* Is the interview scheme broad enough so that different opinions will be heard? Has the researcher developed a schedule that allows for alternative explanations of the phenomena under study? (4) *Data analysis:* How will the researcher triangulate the data? What forms of data gathering will be used to ensure that the research is trustworthy? (5) *Data presentation:* What are the policy implications of one's findings? Do the policies naturally derive from the data, or are they the opined conclusions of a subjective reviewer?

Each of these questions needs to be asked—and answered—prior to beginning the research. The strength of ethnographic interviews is that they allow informants to offer insights into their own lives and experiences that are impossible to gather with other instruments. The struggle, however, is that no hard-and-fast rules exist; rather, the research experience must unfold heuristically within the structure outlined in this chapter.

References

Becker, H. S., and Geer, B. "Participant Observation and Interviewing: A Comparison." In W. J. Filstead (ed.), *Qualitative Methodology: Firsthand Involvement with the Social World*. Chicago: Markham, 1972.

Chaffee, E. E., and Tierney, W. G. *Collegiate Culture and Leadership Strategies*. New York: American Council on Education/Macmillan, 1988.

Conklin, H. C. "Ethnography." In D. Sills (ed.), *International Encyclopedia of the Social Sciences*. New York: Macmillan, 1968.

Dill, D. D. "The Management of Academic Culture: Notes on the Management of Meaning and Social Integration." *Higher Education*, 1982, *11*, 303-320.

Geertz, C. *The Interpretation of Cultures*. New York: Basic Books, 1973.

Guba, E. G., and Lincoln, Y. S. *Effective Evaluation: Improving the Usefulness of Evaluation Results Through Responsive and Naturalistic Approaches*. San Francisco: Jossey-Bass, 1981.

Gumport, P. J. "Curricula as Signposts of Cultural Change." *Review of Higher Education*, 1988, *12*, 49-61.

Fetterman, D. M. *Ethnography: Step by Step*. Newbury Park, Calif.: Sage, 1989.

Langness, L. L., and Frank, G. *Lives: An Anthropological Approach to Biography*. Novato, Calif.: Chandler & Sharp, 1981.

Lincoln, Y. S., and Guba, E. G. *Naturalistic Inquiry*. Newbury Park, Calif.: Sage, 1985.

Masland, A. T. "Organizational Culture in the Study of Higher Education." *Review of Higher Education*, 1985, *8*, 157-168.

Moffatt, M. *Coming of Age in New Jersey*. New Brunswick, N.J.: Rutgers University Press, 1989.

Patton, M. Q. *Qualitative Evaluation Methods*. Newbury Park, Calif.: Sage, 1980.

Patton, M. Q. *Practical Evaluation*. Newbury Park, Calif.: Sage, 1982.

Spradley, J. P. *The Ethnographic Interview*. New York: Holt, Rinehart & Winston, 1979.

Spradley, J. P. *Participant Observation*. New York: Holt, Rinehart & Winston, 1980.

Tierney, W. G. "Ethnography: An Alternative Evaluation Methodology." *Review of Higher Education*, 1985, *8*, 93-105.

Tierney, W. G. "Organizational Culture in Higher Education: Defining the Essentials." *Journal of Higher Education*, 1988, *59* (1), 2-21.

Tierney, W. G. *Curricular Landscapes, Democratic Vistas: Transformative Leadership in Higher Education*. New York: Praeger, 1989.

Tierney, W. G. *Official Encouragement, Institutional Discouragement: Minorities in Academe*. Norwood, N.J.: Ablex, in press.

William G. Tierney is associate professor of education and senior research associate in the Center for the Study of Higher Education, The Pennsylvania State University, University Park.

Internal auditing is both an art and a science. It is designed to improve effectiveness and efficiency and to protect an institution's assets. Many of the concepts and techniques used to analyze institutions of higher education are qualitative in nature and suited to institutional research.

Auditing as Institutional Research: A Qualitative Focus

David M. Fetterman

Internal auditing is the art and science of describing and testing checks and balances in institutional management. It requires detailed study of departments and functions to improve effectiveness and efficiency and to protect the institution's assets. Many of the techniques used to analyze institutions of higher education are qualitative in nature—notably, participant observation, informal interviews, triangulation, and solicitation of the insider's point of view. Properly conducted, internal auditing in higher education facilitates the academic mission.

This discussion presents the many types of internal audits, including fiscal, operational, electronic data processing, investigative (dealing with fraud or embezzlement), and management consulting. In addition, a new form of auditing is on the horizon: ethnographic auditing. Each approach tests internal controls or mechanisms. Some approaches are broad in focus, others are narrow. However, each relies on both qualitative and quantitative techniques to achieve its goals. This chapter focuses on the qualitative techniques that internal auditors routinely employ.

Fiscal Audit

The foundation of most auditing is a fiscal review. Does the department or function have a budget? Do the figures add up? Does the system ensure a separation of duties between employees who accept funds and those who record and balance funds? Fiscal auditing is primarily concerned with the books and is conducted to ensure that the department accurately represents its stated self-worth. On the simplest level, a review of petty cash constitutes a basic part of a fiscal audit. A count of the funds and a review of the receipts provide an excellent baseline for determining the financial integrity of the petty cash fund and its custodian. In addition, an informal interview with the custodian of the fund and his or her supervisor sheds some light on actual practice. Does the supervisor periodically check on the custodian? Does the custodian approve the supervisor's reimbursement receipts? If so, are the custodian and supervisor aware of the conflict of interest involved? Has the supervisor considered having the reimbursement receipts approved by his or her own supervisor? These kinds of questions constitute the common-sense, qualitative approach required to protect petty cash funds effectively. A qualitative approach is holistic and contextual. It attempts to look at the whole picture and to place it in a broader social context. Examination of the petty cash fund from a holistic and contextual orientation reveals the cyclical nature of the department's funds as they are routinely used and replenished. In fact, from this perspective there is nothing petty about petty cash. Over time, hundreds of thousands of dollars can pass through a single custodian's hands.

Operational Audit

An operational audit subsumes a fiscal audit and builds on it by focusing on an operation's effectiveness and efficiency. Operational audits focus on such topics as supervision, communication, planning, and analysis, as well as such mundane topics as equipment inventories and petty cash.

An operational audit differs from a fiscal audit in both scope and interpretation. For example, an operational audit of a department requires the same kind of review of petty cash as conducted in a fiscal audit. However, an operational review brings the determination about the status of the petty cash fund to a higher level of analysis. A finding about petty cash would be combined with other findings to determine if a pattern existed, such as sloppy management practices. In other words, a problem with the handling of a department's petty cash would be viewed as a potential manifestation of a larger management problem.

Operational audits take more time than do fiscal audits, but they provide a much richer picture of an organization's management. Such audits use both qualitative and quantitative data but require a qualitative review of all quantitative data. A classic audit reviews a department's management information systems. The first questions to ask in this case are traditional audit questions that happen to be qualitative in nature: Do you have a management information system? If so, can I look at it? The auditor must analyze the quality of the quantitative data in the management information system to determine whether management is relying on valid, reliable, and hopefully useful information to make its decisions. Poor-quality data results in poor decisions in even the most sophisticated management information or decision-making systems.

During one audit of a university hospital pharmacy, participant observation was a useful qualitative technique. It involved informally interviewing and observing pharmacists, attempting to solicit their perspectives about their jobs. The technique revealed the pharmacists' belief that the workload statistics used in the pharmacy were a joke because the system of recording productivity data did not accurately reflect the pharmacists' behavior. The workload system merely counted the number of prescriptions to measure productivity—a misleading measure because one prescription might take two minutes to prepare, whereas another prescription might require half an hour or an hour. Supervisors set schedules and established unrealistic productivity standards based on this information. The system was a clear case of garbage in, garbage out (see Fetterman, 1986, 1990, for detailed discussions of this study).

In another operational audit, the department under review used a computer spreadsheet to track its income and expenses, a major improvement over the back-of-the-envelope system too many departments rely on. However, an analysis of the formulas in the spreadsheet revealed an error. Masked by the appearance of a computer's technical accuracy, the error was compounded in being repeated week after week, month after month, year after year. An unobtrusive review of the quality of the quantitative data in the spreadsheet saved the institution real money.

A third operational audit revealed that although a department was conscientiously and accurately placing data in the management information system, no one ever looked at the data in aggregate or attempted to sort them in any fashion. This audit finding suggested poor planning and analysis, because decision makers did not use a valuable source of information. The findings of these three examples largely derived from qualitative forms of inquiry: observing and participating in the lives of employees, conducting informal interviews, soliciting the insider's viewpoint, and analyzing the quality of quantitative data (see Fetterman, 1988, 1989, for detailed reviews of qualitative techniques and concepts).

The operational auditor communicates with clients throughout the audit. Clients have numerous opportunities to comment on preliminary perceptions and findings. The auditor asks the client questions verbally, through memoranda and electronic mail, and in draft reports. This process enables the client to provide input and the auditor to revise continually his or her understanding and assessment of the system. This interactive approach is typical of qualitative research. It brings the auditor close to the clients' perceptions of their program. It also increases the accuracy and usefulness of the findings, making the information directly relevant to program personnel. The clients are thus more likely to implement the auditor's recommendations to improve the program.

Electronic Data-Processing Audit

An electronic data-processing audit focuses on mainframe and personal computer security controls. The auditor asks questions such as the following: Are users required to use and update passwords? Is access to sensitive records such as payroll information limited? Does the department have written and updated documentation about a given system? Do employees back up their data and programs in case of system failure? Most of these questions can be answered simply by asking individual employees, conducting tests, and reviewing existing documentation. An employee may claim to back up the data but be unable to provide any backup disks. Or another employee may be able to produce a string of cases in which data were lost. A classic qualitative approach—triangulation—involves comparing what people say with what they do, or, more broadly, comparing many sources to determine the accuracy of a given piece of information. Behavior is an excellent source of evidence in any triangulation effort.

Investigative Audit

The investigative audit focuses on suspicions or allegations of fraud and abuse. Allegations cover a wide range of activities: An employee may routinely receive a payroll check for a nonexistent or ghost employee. A faculty member may be consulting in excess of the amount allowable under university policy and procedure. An employee may allege intimidation by management. Investigations in each of these areas rely heavily on qualitative approaches, including informal interviews, use of key informants, and unobtrusive reviews of archival material such as calendars, travel reimbursements, and electronic mail.

In the case of an alleged ghost employee, for example, informal interviews with the complainant co-worker may provide a wealth of information, although interview information alone is rarely sufficient. However, it is invaluable in building a model of the event. Informal interviews may provide sufficient detail about the situation to document it and to confront the individual and ameliorate the problem, or, if necessary, to set up a "sting operation" to catch the individual.

A faculty member may complain about being routinely required to substitute for a supervisor because the supervisor is spending too much time consulting. Telephone calls to consulting agencies and a review of newsletters advertising workshops and calendars can reveal a tremendous amount of information about the individual's activities. In one case, a faculty member's calendar had so many requests for colleagues to substitute for him that the calendar had no room for any of his regular teaching and research activities. This same researcher maintained a list of all his consulting activities on his computer. The computer listed the date and time he worked on any activity. These data provided useful documentation, specifying the precise amount of consulting in a given period, including during regular work hours.

A controversial case about an employee who charged management with intimidation required a series of sensitive exchanges. Informal and formal interviews provided insight into the employee's perspective about the incident. The employee's perception was as important as so-called objective reality: individuals act on their perceptions, and their actions have real consequences. Moreover, in this particular case, a detailed review of the actions of the vice-president above the employee's supervisor provided documentation to support the employee's allegation. Informal interviews with the vice-president also supported the allegations—but provided an explanation as well. The vice-president was concerned that the employee was a zealot and was abusing his position, and she believed that she was entitled to come down hard on someone whom she perceived as insubordinate and misguided. The case study description of this somewhat convoluted event was in itself a valuable finding. This information provided management with a basis for dealing with a highly charged, political problem. The practices of verifying and confirming the information enabled management to rectify the situation.

Management Consulting Audit

Management consulting is typically performed at the request of senior management. The audit provides management with information and advice on the institutional vision and goals and conceptualizes or reconceptualizes the particular problem or program under review. The audit is concerned with internal controls, checks, and balances on a metalevel, rather than on a day-to-day programmatic level. Management consulting may be broad or highly specific, requiring expertise in a narrow field of specialization. A management consultant/auditor can respond to global policy or programmatic concerns, such as the reorganization of a university, school, or department. Or, the management consultant might be brought in to solve a highly technical problem.

A consistently successful auditor in a management consulting role is highly dependent on qualitative concepts and techniques. A conflict-ridden department provides a useful illustration. I was asked to provide insight and advice about a university research administration in a department fraught with turmoil and internal conflict. I interviewed faculty members to determine their level of satisfaction with the research administrators, who provided proposal support and monitored faculty research budgets. I found that some faculty members were happy with the services that they received from the research administration, while other faculty members were disgusted with the complexity of dealing with research administrators and the lack of any meaningful service. Faculty had a strong, vested interest in this problem because their grants supported the research administration infrastructure. I traced compliments and complaints to specific individuals, and a pattern emerged. There were two separate units within the research administration. They were artifacts of historical development, emerging as the faculty departments evolved.

The compliments were consistently associated with the client-service-oriented section of the research administration. This unit served as the faculty members' contact for all problems and concerns in the proposal/grant process. A faculty member with a problem would call the client representative (the research administrator), who would respond promptly to any request. If the research administrator did not know the answer to a question, he or she would research the problem and get back to the faculty member.

The complaints all traced back to the functionally oriented unit. In essence, a separate person was responsible for each of the major elements of a grant or grant proposal. Researchers had to learn whom to work with at each stage of the proposal/grant administration. Many faculty found this process frustrating. Periodically, the entire system would come to a grinding halt when a single research administrator was absent because no one else in the unit could perform that administrator's function. The research administrators had been functioning in this fashion for decades and could not understand why the faculty were not happy with the service that they provided.

My analysis of this complex set of relationships relied heavily on interviews, observation, and participation in the research administrators' lives on a daily basis in order to draw an accurate portrait of their predicament. I knew that senior administrators were considering a merger of the two research administration units. I recommended against it. True, some economies of scale and overall efficiencies could have been accomplished by the merger. But, clearly, the units' cultures in the administrative organization clashed, and a merger would have resulted in even greater turmoil. (The organizational differences had led, historically, to conflicts, turf wars, personal jealousies, and other dysfunctional relationships.) I also recommended that consideration be given to training the functionally oriented unit in client-service-oriented pilot groups to respond to faculty complaints. The functionally oriented unit was concerned about its autonomy, independence, and dignity, and this training enabled its administrators to test the other approach without having it forced down their throats.

A management consultant/auditor also performs highly specific functions, such as writing a proposal for a high-priority program (for example, Upward Bound) or developing a questionnaire for a medical center. Although such tasks are more focused and circumscribed than is an analysis of an organization, they also rely on qualitative approaches. In the first example, informal and formal networks are essential to the job of building a proposal team. Informal interviews with the sponsors, prospective clients, and operational managers help refine the proposal and ensure that it reflects their needs and concerns. This type of effort is vital to a strongly competitive proposal. Similarly, in the second example, informal interviews with both the medical center managers and prospective recipients before the construction of a questionnaire can ensure that the questionnaire elicits relevant information and that the questions are phrased in a language and format that is meaningful to all parties.

Ethnographic Audit

Ethnographic auditing—the systematic application of ethnographic techniques and concepts to auditing—is a relatively new development in the field. Ethnographic auditing highlights the roles of culture, subculture, values, rituals, and physical environment in higher education and views the institution as a living, breathing organism with its own life cycle. In addition, this approach demonstrates the economic consequences of adopting various philosophical orientations or worldviews and clarifies the role of information systems, the value of data bases for decision making, and the roles of judgment and honesty in management. Ethnographic auditing relies on the application of a host of qualitative approaches such as participant observation, key-informant interviews, informal interviews, triangulation, solicitation of the insider's perspective, and conceptualization of a unit as a sociocultural system (see Fetterman, 1990, for a detailed discussion of ethnographic auditing in higher education; and Fetterman, 1989, for a detailed presentation of ethnography).

One of the most effective tools in ethnographic auditing is the case study. Case studies describe a department as a community, subculture, or human organism. A department has its own rules of behavior, norms, economic systems, power structures, and status symbols and its own identifiable character or ethos. Case studies provide a detailed picture of the human organization, communication, and value system of a department or school. This type of description places individual interactions into a larger context of historical circumstances and illuminates the politics of daily interaction in a department. One of the simplest ways of illustrating the ethnographic auditing approach is to present a case study of a department found on almost every campus: the library.

Library Audit

I was asked to study and evaluate a university research library by one of the library directors. The overall assessment was not positive. A number of problems warranted attention, ranging from a poor conception of the institutional mission to conflicting worldviews and value systems among the staff.

The core of the problem was that the library had a weak and fragmented cultural system. Employees had no central conception of purpose. The librarians had lost their mission in a maze of departments and of processing and cataloging rules and regulations. The ethnographic audit findings helped to revitalize the library's cultural system by reminding management and staff members of their mission. The auditors provided a simple mechanical model of library operations to assist library staff in defining their purpose. In essence, the ethnographic audit attempted to make explicit the library's implicit cultural rules and values.

The technical services part of a library, for example, is actually a complex production system. A volume passes through a series of conversion processes, and the processing is complete when the volume is placed on the library shelves for use. The output is a properly bound, cataloged volume, physically accessible to a user. Of course, many subroutines exist within each component of the system's flow pattern. However, the section's basic mission—putting that volume on the shelf for the user—was the cultural thread that held them together.

In this fragmented cultural system, each department and subunit represented a subculture. The library's poorly defined cultural system was confounded by subcultural conflict. "All companies have subcultures, because functional differences . . . single out special aspects of the business environment. . . . Each has its own relevant environment and world view; special heroes, rituals, ceremonies, language, and symbols communicate particular values. Subcultures can shape beliefs and determine behaviors in much the same way that culture can" (Deal and Kennedy, 1982, p. 151).

From an audit or evaluation perspective, the library management paid insufficient attention to the efficient coordination of production operation details and the summative effect of a unit's or department's processes and procedures on the whole system. Translated into cultural language, the subcultures clashed and produced maladaptive behavior patterns: low morale and low productivity. This problem was discovered by using such techniques as key-informant interviews, informal interviews, semi-autobiographical interviews, archival materials, and listening to the library "folktales" that various librarians told.

The original cataloger librarians represented the most vocal and antimainstream subculture. They provided detailed accounts of what they perceived as personal injustices inflicted on them by management. They had their own heroes who had won grievances against the library administration. The folktales generated from these events highlighted the employees' individual complaints. Heroic figures in the subculture proved to be extremely articulate key informants, providing vivid and often extensively documented accounts of their lives in the library. Their autobiographical accounts focused on their professional clashes with management. Archival data, such as newspaper articles, were also useful in documenting the problem. Many librarians had repeatedly voiced their displeasure with management in the campus newspaper over the years. They described the working climate as oppressive and hostile. In addition, an overwhelming number of grievances stemmed from this subculture. The grievance documents represented another useful archival data source with which to triangulate individual reports. Interviews with management were valuable in placing the clash of subcultures in an institutional context. Management was attuned to this problem because they had for several years perceived the cataloger subculture as ripe for unionization.

"Subcultures can be very destructive in weak cultural environments. When the corporation's values are impossible to understand, a subculture can dictate behavior, and eventually cause a sort of cultural drift in the company" (Deal and Kennedy, 1982, p. 152). Library staff members and management shared few values. In fact, value conflict was epidemic and manifest in myriad dysfunctional behaviors. For example, from a management perspective, data for decision making were fundamental. In the library, each department and subunit had its own separate information system, but there was not an overall information system to collect, aggregate, and monitor productivity data systematically and comprehensively. Many diverse professional forms and data sheets circulated throughout the library. A cursory review suggested that the elaborate data collection system was effective. After a few informal interviews with the librarians, however, I learned of their frustrations with the data collection system. Because they worked in discrete units or departments, they were unable to identify the source of the problem. I viewed the system holistically and attempted to track books through the entire system. I observed immediately that the forms used to collect statistics did not reflect management's information needs. One section of the library aggregated copy, original, and variant-edition categories into a single category: titles. This practice hid the variation within each category—information that is necessary to identify where a production problem exists. This type of problem was endemic to the entire system.

I recommended a management information system, including well-defined goals and objectives (including numerical goals), input and output data to measure work flow, consistent output standards, a measuring device to determine how staff members allocated their time to complete tasks, a feedback signal or monitoring component to evaluate their progress toward specific goals, and a protocol for corrective action (Garrett and Silver, 1966). I also recommended that management attempt to support the various subcultures rather than waste time attempting to crush specific ones. I believed that it was important to "encourage each subculture to enrich its own cultural life. Rather than be afraid of subcultures pulling apart, a symbolic manager will seek to strengthen each subculture as an effective cabal within the overall culture. Thus, he or she will often attend functions called to celebrate a particular subculture; participate in special awards for the heroes of the subculture; and generally endorse the subculture's existence and meaning within the larger culture" (Deal and Kennedy, 1982, p. 153).

Committees formed of members from various subcultures joined to address common problems. This meeting served to sensitize them to each other's concerns and problems. The emphasis was on using subcultures to enrich the larger culture. The effectiveness of this recommendation was limited by the weakness of the existing cultural system. However, it successfully reduced the existing tension for a majority of the library subcultures.

The supervision system also needed improvement in the library. The most significant areas of weakness involved standards of performance and evaluation and span of supervisory control over staff. The standards of performance and evaluation criteria were not explicit or commonly understood, leading to inconsistent appraisals and misevaluations and resulting in what appeared to be inappropriate terminations. "If people tend to see the firing as arbitrary and unfair, they become confused and upset. In one fell swoop, the culture is called into question" (Deal and Kennedy, 1982, p. 73).

The lack of clearly established and mutually agreed upon goals and standards unnecessarily exposes management to charges of perceived inequities or capricious decision making. Once consistency and the foundation of due process are established, rituals are useful tools to ameliorate the untoward effects of appropriate but uncomfortable transitions. These rituals can range from annual performance appraisals to retirement banquets. "To bring these disturbing events under control, sophisticated companies provide elaborate rites. The rituals not only provide security during an unwanted transition but also put the culture on display and dramatize and reinforce its values and beliefs. Those managers who don't consider the dramatic aspects of a transition ritual will miss an opportunity to use it to extend the culture's influence" (Deal and Kennedy, 1982, p. 73).

The problem of supervision was clearly linked to poor leadership. A brief historical review, based on archival data such as employment records and informal interviews, revealed a high degree of turnover in management positions. According to one of the library directors, the circumstances included four changes in one department in less than five years, a change in a senior management position four years prior to my audit, and three changes within the same time period in one of the most sensitive or volatile subdepartments. In addition, two other senior managers were new to the library. The high rate of turnover resulted in a lack of continuity in leadership and in management expectations of staff member performance. This lack of continuity in turn led to staff concerns and an unclear understanding of their roles.

An ethnographic auditor views the physical environment as part of the cultural system. In the production part of the library, workspace was not conducive to an efficient production work flow. The limited space available was poorly organized. Equipment was located in areas that were either difficult to access or inappropriate. In addition, the lack of privacy, the noise, and the poor lighting and air circulation were not conducive to efficient operations. This atmosphere contrasted with the plush new offices of the public service librarians, who worked with students and professors at the reference desk, at the computer terminals, and in the stacks. "Differences in the way physical sites are arranged for different classes of employees is one sure sign of a weak or fragmented culture" (Deal and Kennedy, 1982, pp. 130–131).

Participant observation was instrumental in sensitizing me to these problems in the physical environment. I studied the library culture for more than six months. I was involved in the daily lives of staff members, interviewing them every day, eating lunch with them, and periodically helping them with an acquisition or cataloging task. The validity of their complaints about workspace inadequacies was easy to verify during daily observation and participation in their work lives. Overall, the inequitable (and disorganized) work station arrangement compounded the cultural disarray in the organization. All these maladaptive patterns impeded productivity.

In addition, I took time to interview librarians at various comparable research libraries throughout the United States and learned that the conflict between librarians who work in the production sections and those who work with faculty, including the physical manifestations in workspace conditions, is typical within the larger research library culture. Nevertheless, because an ethnographic auditor is a change agent who attempts to move the organization beyond the status quo, the findings in my case study led me to recommend extensive renovations of the workspace (now completed) to eliminate the vast discrepancy between the plush surroundings of one group of librarians and the "sweatshop" conditions of another group. In this particular case, the results of ethnographic auditing vividly captured senior management's attention.

Conclusion

Audits have many forms and faces. However, they are an instrumental but often neglected source of institutional research in higher education. The various auditing approaches presented in this chapter typically combine both quantitative and qualitative techniques. The discussion here focused on the qualitative concepts and techniques that are indispensable in internal audit work. All forms of auditing use qualitative approaches in one fashion or another. However, some approaches, such as management consulting and ethnographic auditing, rely on qualitative approaches more than do financial or electronic data-processing audits. Qualitative approaches are not a panacea in the pursuit of institutional research. However, they are invaluable tools in the institutional researcher's arsenal and help the researcher to make sense of often chaotic and conflict-ridden environments.

References

Deal, T. E., and Kennedy, A. A. *Corporate Cultures: The Rites and Rituals of Corporate Life.* Reading, Mass.: Addison-Wesley, 1982.

Fetterman, D. M. "Operational Auditing in a Teaching Hospital: A Cultural Approach." *Internal Auditor,* 1986, *43* (2), 48–54.

Fetterman, D. M. (ed.). *Qualitative Approaches to Evaluation in Education: The Silent Scientific Revolution.* New York: Praeger, 1988.

Fetterman, D. M. *Ethnography: Step by Step.* Newbury Park, Calif.: Sage, 1989.

Fetterman, D. M. "Ethnographic Auditing: A New Approach to Evaluating Management." In W. B. Tierney (ed.), *Assessing Academic Climates and Cultures.* New Directions for Institutional Research, no. 68. San Francisco: Jossey-Bass, 1990.

Garrett, L., and Silver, M. *Production Management Analysis.* (2nd ed.) San Diego, Calif.: Harcourt Brace Jovanovich, 1966.

David M. Fetterman is administrator and professor of education at Stanford University, Stanford, California, and Sierra Nevada College, Incline Village, Nevada. He is also president of the American Anthropological Association's Council on Anthropology and Education.

Portfolios allow a full range of outcome considerations that enhance both the development of individual students and the development of curricula.

Capturing the Richness of Student Outcomes with Qualitative Techniques

Mary Anne Bunda

Offices of institutional research are seen as the technical support for central decision makers in higher education. They have long provided the grist for enrollment planning and staffing needs within the institution and have served as well as the primary reporters to outside audiences. Pressures from both internal and external agents have now forced institutional researchers into the realm of curricular evaluation at all levels of the institution. One of the most serious problems for the institutional researcher arises from efforts to aid departments in majors assessment. Faculty see the determination of curriculum as solely their responsibility. Departments tend to view the demands for assessment as intrusions on their normal practice. The institutional research office must be seen as a facilitator of the task and not as an outside evaluator for either the state or the central administration.

Curriculum Assessment Strategies

A number of different majors assessment strategies have been developed that are consistent with the different views of the goals of assessment. As Halpern (1985) has pointed out, there are essentially three different views of the ends of assessment: program improvement, gatekeeping at the course or degree level, and budgeting and accountability. These goals focus the use of assessment results on the curriculum, the student, or the budgetary allocations. The three goals can be held simultaneously on any campus when associated with a specific procedure or strategy, but one goal eventually becomes dominant because the focus of data use for each goal is different. Indeed, the foci are different enough to preclude multiple uses.

35

If assessment is used either for internal or statewide budgetary allocations, the need for a single common index across all disciplinary or departmental units forces constraints on any single department's procedure. The procedures so narrowly focus assessment that the information is not useful for either program development or student advisement. When assessment is characterized solely as a gatekeeping function, there is a presumption that the learning experiences provided for students are adequate and that assessment ensures that students have sufficiently taken advantage of course offerings. If the instrument is used to deny an academic credential to students, it is essential that each of the elements that appears on the instrument is related to a planned learning experience of students. Consequently, material related to planned electives is not included on a gatekeeping measure. Additionally, gatekeeping procedures are introduced too late in a student's academic career to provide timely input.

Dissatisfaction with single-core measures of student learning in the major has led some institutions to use the senior project or comprehensive examination as a gatekeeping device. The senior project requires the student to work independently in a self-selected area of the major field. While the benefits to the individual student are threefold—a deepening understanding of the discipline, the opportunity for independent study, and synthesis within the discipline—it is not clear how this activity can be aggregated across all students to enlighten the faculty concerning the core learning that takes place within the courses. This activity benefits the individual student only; it does not inform the curriculum review process. The comprehensive examination, on the other hand, does not provide the opportunity for independent study and is just as expensive in terms of faculty time. Faculty must not only grade the examinations, but each must be tailored to the specific planned program. Information provided to the student at the end of a college career is dubious at best.

If an assessment strategy is to be developed for a curriculum improvement goal, it must provide not only an adequate information base to make judgments about the entire curriculum but also information valuable to the development of individual students. Focus on this goal of assessment requires that the measures or procedures be designed with the common elements of the curriculum in mind, but also with the unique emphasis that each student designs in an academic program through his or her selection of electives. In other words, in order to be successful, a strategy must inform decisions concerning an individual student and the program as a whole. The standards developed for the judgment of assessment programs by accrediting agencies require benefits of assessment to the institution rather than to the student. (The notable exception here is Alverno College; see Mentkowski and Loacker, 1985).

Curriculum design decisions involve much more than changing a single course or adding a new experience. "There is a notable absence of structure and coherence in college and university curricula. Our analysis indicates a continued fragmentation of an educational experience that ought to be greater than the sum of its parts" (Zemsky, 1989, p. 7). While fragmentation generally refers to the problem of liberal or general education, there is growing evidence that learned societies have concern for the "breadth—especially interrelating content"—within the major ("Study-in-Depth . . . ," 1990). The curriculum design data are applied to a host of learning opportunities that the department provides for students. In a major, changes can be made in the structure of required courses, permitted areas of electives and prerequisites, or a wide range of out-of-class activities that are offered to students in the forms of extracurricular clubs, colloquia, and outside speakers. No faculty member believes that the development of a student is restricted to in-class activities (Steele, 1989). Assessment data must not simply address course outcomes. The assessment techniques used may collect data on the usefulness of out-of-class activities in order to enrich the total learning environment.

Assessment activities are supposed to be an illuminating source of information that allows faculty to make decisions about the curricula. The limited practice of assessing and tinkering with a small part of the curriculum may not solve the problem. An assessment system that is designed to search for a synthesis of experience for each student as well as the achievement of specific outcomes may ease the fragmentation in the programs. This type of assessment strategy must be linked to all of the aspects of an academic program, whether delivered through courses or not.

Faculty use a wide range of recommendations to design curricular experiences, for example, recommendations from scholarly societies, accrediting agencies, and specialists within the department. The promise of assessment is that it will provide the faculty with another source of information to use in the curriculum development process. The structure of the assessment strategies must be similar to the structure of learning experiences—continuous and individually designed while growing in complexity as the student learns more about the discipline, but also incorporating elements common to all students. The development of a portfolio of achievement by each student, based on departmental definitions, can satisfy the needs of both the individual student and the departmental faculty.

The Fine Arts as a Case Study

The complexity of course offerings and desired outcomes in the majors offered in higher education can be seen easily in the fine arts. The evaluation of achievement in the fine arts presents a more complex problem than is encountered in any of the other disciplines. Some people believe that the use of any evaluative process within the arts is impossible because of an inherent lack of objectivity, and that "the collective statistical method is not suited for opinions and judgments regarding the arts" (Christy, 1948, p. 11). Additionally, pursuit of an academic major in one of the fine arts at a university is different from the study of that art at a conservatory. Generally speaking, both types of institution conduct some sort of assessment with a required senior recital or showing in the student's specialty as an exit procedure and have gatekeeping assessments such as auditions upon entry. But universities and colleges provide students with a much broader study of the area of the arts and generally relate the students' specialties to other aspects of their college careers. For instance, theater majors have experience in set decoration, lighting, and directing as well as performance. Assessment strategies used to make decisions concerning individual students at the university, therefore, are more complex than a simple senior recital, although the judgment of artistic performance is never a simple matter. The strategy must provide a student with the opportunity to show his or her development across the breadth of the art form as well as his or her excellence in a specialty. But in both types of institution much of the instruction in the specialty occurs one to one, the master teacher slowly shaping the student's performance on the basis of evaluative information (Colwell, 1970).

Both universities and conservatories must deal with the issue of defining the quality of an artistic performance. Any definition of art is by the nature of the subject open to argument (Barrett, 1979). The problem of evaluating student products is curricular as well as aesthetic (Eisner and Ecker, 1966). Not only must the faculty be able to provide adequate feedback to the individual student, but they also must be able to use those judgments of students' work to make judgments about the curriculum. While all of the fine arts have goals that are easy to measure quantitatively, such as purely cognitive knowledge or purely technical skill, in no case would faculty want to make decisions about the requirements of the major for all students only in these two areas. Consequently, assessment strategies that are designed to address only a limited set of options are viewed with great suspicion. However, technical skill is systematically monitored and knowledge of the history and fundamentals of the art form is seen as essential to upper-division work.

In addition to the complex nature of outcomes in the fine arts, the learning experiences of a major are explicitly different from those of the traditional academic disciplines. Programs in the arts tend to encourage, and often require, students to participate in out-of-class experiences where they can practice and enhance their crafts, for example, the university symphony orchestra, the graphics department of the school newspaper, and the university theater production company. Performance in these extracurricular activities should be considered in terms of development of the individual student and in terms of contribution to the curriculum as a whole. Changes in out-of-class requirements are just as serious as changes in course syllabi or course requirements.

Programs of study for individual students that include out-of-class experiences are designed on the basis of information collected by a faculty adviser. The information collected concerning any one student should not be collected after a program of study is completed. Very often students are required to take an annual look at the development of their performance capabilities. Faculty are not only interested in performance at the end of an academic program but also interested in tracking a student throughout his or her program. Much of the advanced work of a student is individualized with a master teacher. The method that most fine arts departments have developed for tracking individual development is portfolio construction and assessment. Students and advisers discuss the contents of the portfolios as they develop the learning experience plan or the individual curriculum. While the adviser is likely initially to aid the student in selection of work, a key element in the use of portfolios is that students are responsible for the selection of the products. For instance, a beginning dance student may have faculty assistance in the selection of a tap number for the portfolio after year one, whereas an advanced student would be expected to review all of the video segments in his or her portfolio and substitute where necessary. The selection of one product over another requires that the student develop the skill of self-assessment. Programs in the arts often have as an explicit goal the development of self-assessment skill ("Outcomes Assessment . . . ," 1990, p. 3). Without successive portfolios to review, the faculty adviser or master teacher cannot see whether students are developing the skill of self-assessment.

The portfolio is similar to the senior project in that it serves as an excellent tool with which to foster the development of an individual student. Portfolios in music, theater, and dance show much more about skill than does the senior recital. The portfolio shows the scope of the work that the student has accomplished. Likewise, the portfolio of an art student contains more than the specialized media of a senior show. It includes works (or photographs of works) in media outside of the specialty. There is no reason to restrict the construction and assessment of a portfolio to the senior year. Students may be held responsible for the annual submission of a revised portfolio. Typically, departments do not analyze a student's development across portfolios, but since all students can have samples in the portfolio that show a particular skill, aggregation across the portfolio is possible. Also, review of portfolios constructed at a particular point in an academic career can focus attention on learning stages. While selection of criteria for the contents of the portfolio is clearly a matter for the individual department, because the criteria are based on the goals of the program, there are lessons that all academic units can learn from this strategy for assessment. Consideration of the portfolio is as continuous as the growth of the student in the art form.

Portfolio Elements. The development of a portfolio should not be confused with the construction of a scrapbook of scholarly or academic memorabilia. Nor is the portfolio a transcript indicating the academic record of the student. Portfolios are designed to display the best work of a person, not to document each experience (Nielsen, 1984). Portfolios are used by professionals in a variety of careers as a means of showing examples of their work to prospective employers. The portfolio documents the strengths of the person along dimensions that are agreed upon as important in the profession. Prospective employers know that they are not reviewing a random sample of the person's work. As an assessment tool, portfolios help document the best work of the student along all of the dimensions of interest for a department. But an academic portfolio is different from an employment portfolio because it is linked to the program goals of the department. Employment portfolios are limited to an individual's specialty.

The dimensions of interest in an academic portfolio are defined by the scope of the discipline addressed by the program. While each of the dimensions is addressed in the structure of the department's program it is not necessary for a course to be uniquely dedicated to the dimension. Several courses may address the dimension, or it may be covered in only part of a course. The products themselves may be part of a course experience or may be produced specifically for the portfolio or while participating in some extracurricular event. The products required as part of a portfolio reflect the definition of the discipline or art that the department uses in the conception of its program. The portfolio functions as a synthesizing device for the student as successive portfolios are developed throughout an academic career. The student is able to see the discipline as a whole as it is represented by personal effort. The specifications of the products in the portfolio are as broad or as narrow as the department has defined the discipline. For instance, it may be perfectly reasonable for one dance department to require a video of choreographed work by a student, while another department does not. One theater department may want samples of improvisation, while another requires samples of set decoration. The goals of the program define the exact nature of the specifications; however, some general guidelines for the development are listed below.

Cognitive Component. Each department has specific nonperformance objectives for all students in the program. Generally, these objectives relate to the history of the art form and its relation to society as a whole or to the humanities. These objectives can be measured by a test of cognitive learning. While some of the arts have nationally available standardized devices (for example, the music test developed by the Educational Testing Service as part of the Graduate Record Examination program), these instruments can also be constructed by the departmental faculty. The validity of any national test for local objectives is clearly an issue, particularly in cases where the relationship of the art form to society at large is a substantial component of the program. The portfolio guideline for the cognitive component should specify when a student should take the test and whether the test is used as a gatekeeper for any other activity in the program. In most cases, students in the arts complete the fundamentals component of their respective majors during their first two years of study. Some programs may decide to use the test of fundamentals as a gatekeeper for upper-division course work. Other programs may allow students to enter master classes without regard to the cognitive component of the program.

Technique Sample. Each of the arts has a range of specific performance areas in which students develop proficiency. Clearly, in most cases the technique samples will not be paper-and-pencil products. Videotaped and audiotaped performances are likely to be the submission requirements in music, dance, and theater, while art may require either the product itself or slides of the product taken at different, specified angles. All departments are likely to specify a range of samples to represent specific aspects of technique. For instance, an art department may specify a number of media and expressions in three dimensions as well as two (Keiler, 1961). Dance departments may specify a number of styles to be demonstrated, for example, jazz, ethnic, and ballet. Students should be made aware of the range of technique samples at the outset, but the department may phase in the requirement for presentation of the samples across a student's academic career. By phasing in required samples of technique, the department systematically requires a student to reconsider his or her conception of techniques required with the discipline. This exercise is particularly important for students who are in art education curricula. In some cases, departments might use a range definition for the audition portfolio for admission into the program similar to that used for the annual review portfolio. Thus, successive portfolios provide a master teacher with an indication of growth. Inclusion of work in the techniques sample does not preclude the assessment of aesthetic quality of the item, but the sample would be provided primarily because it exemplifies technical skill. Any professional program that has motor skill objectives should be interested in an assessment of technique. For example, in medical programs the ability to give an injection is better assessed directly than indirectly with a paper-and-pencil test.

Breadth Sample. Each of the arts has a range of specific performance areas in which students develop proficiency. For example, a voice major may be required to show samples of work that range from musical comedy to opera, or from solo performances to choral work, no matter what the student's specialty. The breadth criterion is one of the clear differences between study of the arts at the baccalaureate level and study at a conservatory. The breadth criterion specifies those areas in which all students must gain some proficiency. There may be departmental differences with respect to the areas in which the student should develop breadth. The size of the program and the scope of the offerings determine the areas in which the students can reasonably expect to gain proficiency. Clearly, again, this sample will not be restricted to a paper-and-pencil product. However, in this case, the students may include reviews of their works by professors or critics in addition to samples of performance. In many cases, breadth of experience may be represented with material produced outside of the classroom. Theater departments may ask for works in which the student has acted, been the director, designed sets, or designed costumes (Brackett, 1964). In addition to a range of compositions, music departments may request solo performance, small ensemble performance, and large ensemble performance (National Association of Schools of Music, 1985). Some departments may require works that are more applied or interdisciplinary in nature, for example, graphic arts, commercial arts, and marketing of plays. The specification of breadth, while a departmental option, serves to define the particular art for the student. Breadth expands the definition of the major beyond performance in a specialty. It also specifies the curriculum for the department in terms of breadth of exposure rather than simply in terms of pursuit of individual artistic excellence. It allows the student to see the art form as wider than his or her own specialty. Thus, success within the major is clearly more than the judgment of a senior recital or of the sophomore hearing.

Specialty Recital or Showing. While the senior recital or show is a live performance, replicas of the showing may be placed in the final portfolio along with the ratings of the jury. Prior to the final portfolio, the student can include ideas for the recital as discussion items with his or her academic adviser. Thus, the portfolio can also be used as a diagnostic device for planning by both the student and the faculty adviser. The investment in the construction of the portfolio and the cost of review of the materials are, therefore, not purely expenses of evaluation. Rather, the portfolio serves as a learning or instructional device as well.

Evaluative Uses of the Portfolio. Typically, each student prepares a portfolio for review by his or her master teacher at the end of an academic year. Large programs may have a storage problem, because portfolios often come in very large boxes. Additionally, each adviser must have easy access to video-playback equipment and audio equipment. The portfolio elements are useful in the evaluation of a single student's progress within the major, as well as in the evaluation of the curriculum. As the object of the evaluation varies, the elements of the portfolio are used in different ways. When the portfolio is used by an individual adviser to assess the development of a single student, there is clearly a collaboration between student and adviser in negotiating the meaning of the items in the portfolio. The model for the relationship between the parties is clearly described by Guba and Lincoln (1988) as "naturalistic inquiry." The discussion that takes place generates alternative actions for the student so that areas of perceived weakness can be strengthened. There is an effort by both parties to bring synthesis to the various elements of the portfolio in order to gain an understanding of the student's overall mastery of the area. There is no need for the faculty adviser to quantify the judgment of quality of any of the elements of the portfolio because the discussion with the student can produce a much richer understanding of the quality of the items. However, this is not to say that the adviser does not use artistic judgment in the analysis of the items for the student. The application of aesthetic criteria in evaluating art is a necessary condition for effective teaching (Eisner, 1972). Teacher and student are jointly engaged in qualitative problem solving, which is not a neat progression of steps but rather "a single, continuous means-ends progression" (Ecker, 1966, p. 67). Early analysis of the components of the portfolio helps the student bring the elements of the major into focus. The interaction between the teacher and the student is more important to the development of the individual student than is a quantification of the portfolio at any point in time.

However, when the portfolios of the student body are used for curricular or program evaluation within the major, an effort must be made to quantify the elements of the portfolio as much as possible so that they can be aggregated for the department as a whole or for a sample of students defined by year within the program. Thus, if an adviser makes notes within the portfolio during the advisory session, these notes can later serve as the quantification of judgment. The use of the portfolios for curricular evaluation can be performed throughout the academic year using the files of each master teacher or adviser. Aggregation of evidence can be targeted to specific questions. The cognitive element of the portfolio can be analyzed in relation to the qualitative elements, or it can be analyzed independently.

Quantification of the performance elements of the portfolio can also be accomplished by ratings by juries. Ratings of the performance aspects of the portfolios by jury panels are not new to the arts, but they are considerably more expensive than is the judgment of the adviser. The additional expense benefits evaluation only, whereas the adviser ratings can be charged as both an instructional and evaluation cost because the review of the portfolio benefits the instructional program of the student. Unique evaluation costs are not rare in the arts. Performance ratings by auditors are accomplished independently at senior recitals on a regular basis. However, the categories of the ratings may be different in the assessment of the portfolios. For instance, an instrumental performance may be rated independently on tone, intonation, technique, and interpretation during a live performance and rated only on technique as part of the portfolio. Specialists in the ratings of the arts warn about excessive subdivision of the ratings in that the increased complexity of the process may cause the rater's attention to be simultaneously directed toward too many specifics (Whybrew, 1962). Rather than undertake ratings of multiple dimensions of the work, it may be more useful to the department to have different raters give global judgments of the elements. The ratings of individual aspects are more useful to the individual student. The expense of multiple auditors of the portfolio can be justified only if the accuracy of a rater is questioned, for then multiple auditors may be necessary to counter a charge of bias.

Facilitating the Aggregate Use of Portfolio Information. Before the utility of evaluative information can be demonstrated, the questions that faculty have about the curriculum must be identified. Departmental faculty may need the help of a facilitator to work through the aggregate data; but if that information is to serve the purpose of accountability in program review, the institutional researcher must work with the faculty to legitimize the effort. Faculty are comfortable with the portfolio as a tool for student evaluation, but its application to the entire departmental program requires groundwork and continuous support. The identification of focus questions guides the process of quantification of the judgments of performance. Faculty should establish focus questions for assessment of the curriculum. These questions focus the review of the portfolio. After a few questions are identified, the data can be reviewed for possible leads or hunches. The data then become part of the problem-solving strategies used by the faculty. The qualitative problem-solving mode uses the data to generate additional questions about the curriculum, which then generate additional foci for the portfolio review or the collection of subsidiary data. A problem-solving process is established rather than a single loop of data collection and judgment.

Generating the Initial Question List. Sometimes faculty, even in the arts, think about curricular change only in terms of the alteration of individual syllabi or the addition of new course requirements. Analysis of the portfolios should be guided by a set of revision questions broader than "Which course should be changed?" It is important for the faculty to see that portfolio analysis will not intrude on the evaluation of specific courses taught by individual faculty members. Assessment strategies are only as good as the use made of the information. Faculty must own and trust assessment if it is to be politically viable. If the department is concerned that academic freedom will be breached, help should be given to ensure that the data are coded without identification of individual courses. If no course can be identified, no professor will be asked to change the specific instructional strategies used in the course. Thus, the academic freedom of each professor is preserved.

Additionally, it should be made clear from the outset that the portfolios will not be the only information needed to address the questions of the assessment. The curricular plan may be a "folktale" (Fetterman, 1989) in the department. Requirements and sequences of courses may have been developed on the basis of rationales clear two decades ago, but undocumented for today's students and faculty. Faculty should be encouraged to collect information about the process or to document the process in addition to the outcomes. Documentation can occur with observational techniques such as unobtrusive measures. Indeed, some changes in the curriculum may result simply from faculty looking at the documentation of a process of which they were unaware. For instance, if the faculty were initially to develop a set of questions about the sophomore hearing process— How do students sign up for the hearing? When do they sign up? Who passes the hearing? How many attempts are needed to pass?—they would find that they need exact course completion information about students as they tried to refine the question about when students should sign up. Suppose that most faculty believe that students complete twelve hours of individual study prior to the hearing. Even though no rule exists about twelve hours, faculty believe that departmental culture has set this standard. Upon reviewing course completions, the faculty could decide whether a formal statement of course requirements is necessary.

The initial set of questions to guide the use of the portfolio as an assessment tool can be generated in a brainstorming session of a faculty meeting. The faculty need help in the generation of "grand tour" questions (Fetterman, 1989). As preparation for the initial question-generating meeting, a summary of the portfolios should be constructed. The summary can be derived from the ratings or scores that typically are part of portfolios. Spreadsheet programs (if the information is numerical) or data management programs (if the information is text) are helpful in the manipulation of the information. Given that portfolios are created by students at the end of each academic year, questions can be generated in five categories: (1) audition or admissions—questions that lead either to a change in admissions criteria or to consultation with secondary schools, (2) end of year one—questions that focus on an understanding of either the breadth criterion or technical skill acquisition, (3) end of year two—questions that focus on mastery of the fundamental and possible changes in the didactic instruction, (4) end of year three—questions that focus on either variations of artistic quality across the breadth elements or the kinds of extracurricular activities in which students seem to be concentrating, and (5) end of year four—questions that focus on program review and accountability. Some of the questions may be very detailed, while others may be quite open-ended. It is important to keep the questions inclusionary rather than exclusionary. Boundaries should not be set on the investigation too early. After the generation of new questions is completed, discussion is needed about the criticality of the questions, the process or curricular element that each addresses, and the ability of the faculty to in fact change that process or element. Questions that address universitywide issues such as admissions criteria or liberal education may not be the best with which to begin. While the answers to any and all of the questions may be interesting, it is important to ask which questions will bring action with respect to the curriculum. The question can then lead to a design for quantification of the portfolio and documentation of the curricular process.

Aesthetic and Technical Competence Judgments of Portfolio Material. The kind of questions that the department generates will to some degree direct the kind of judgments made of the performance samples in the portfolios. Given that quantification may be relevant only to the current curricular questions, there is no need to restrict the process to a single set of permanent rules. As the questions focus on different components or stages of the curriculum, the department may select a different method of quantification. However, if the quantification is to be used in a program review system or as part of an accountability system, the institutional research office should work with the department to design a single method for accountability purposes only, which can be used in addition to the curriculum-focused methods. However, the system for quantification for accountability should not be designed until the comments in the portfolios have been analyzed. The system should be reviewed annually to ensure accuracy and fairness.

Essentially, there are three styles of documentation that can be used. First, when the focus questions do not exist, departments may consider the notes of advisers in the portfolios as text for content analysis. Analysis of the notes will produce a summary of areas that advisers have discussed with their students. Disaggregation of these comments by student year will highlight any concentration of concerns with particular techniques or areas of breadth. This task can be accomplished by a single faculty member assigned to curricular evaluation. Second, summary judgments can be produced by each faculty member during meetings with students. Third, multiple judgments of particular aspects of the breadth component can be produced. For instance, the evaluation questions could focus on the breadth elements in the portfolios of third-year students. The department could ask the advisers to globally rate each of the elements in the breadth component for a specific sample of their own advisees, in addition to rating the breadth elements of other advisers' students. This would produce two independent ratings of each portfolio in the sample. An analysis of the level of the rating on the elements in the breadth component and the differences between the ratings would give the department information about common standards and areas of perceived weaknesses.

Portfolios in Other Disciplines. There is clear applicability of this technique of portfolio assessment to all of the academic programs of the university. The portfolio serves as an excellent vehicle for monitoring student progress and initiating synthesis within a field of study. Many of the professional programs will find that portfolios free them to use documentation media beyond print. Additionally, specification of the breadth component can prevent premature specialization at the undergraduate level. Analysis of the elements in the breadth area in addition to provision for a senior project assures synthesis by the students. Additionally, as material is prepared for a portfolio outside of the classroom, there is an integration of learning experiences that are course-related and extracurricular.

Portfolios allow a student to prepare work that is individual in nature but also responsive to the core requirements of the major. The products in the portfolio clearly indicate the personal aspects of learning. Moreover, the products are direct results of a particular aspect of the academic program that may or may not be a formal course. Products can be prepared as part of an extracurricular activity. Rather than being reductionist in nature, portfolios tend to expand our understanding of both programs and outcomes.

References

Barrett, M. *Art Education.* London: Heinemann Educational Books, 1979.

Brackett, O. G. *The Theatre: An Introduction.* New York: Holt, Rinehart & Winston, 1964.

Christy, V. A. *Evaluation of Choral Music.* New York: Teachers College Press, 1948.

Colwell, R. *The Evaluation of Music Teaching and Learning.* Englewood Cliffs, N.J.: Prentice-Hall, 1970.

Ecker, D. W. "The Artistic Process as Qualitative Problem Solving." In E. W. Eisner and D. W. Ecker (eds.), *Readings in Art Education.* Waltham, Mass.: Blaisdell, 1966.

Eisner, E. W. *Educating Artistic Vision.* New York: Macmillan, 1972.

Eisner, E. W., and Ecker, D. W. (eds.). *Readings in Art Education.* Waltham, Mass.: Blaisdell, 1966.

Fetterman, D. M. *Ethnography: Step by Step.* Newbury Park, Calif.: Sage, 1989.

Guba, E. G., and Lincoln, Y. S. "Do Inquiry Paradigms Imply Inquiry Methodologies?" In D. M. Fetterman (ed.), *Qualitative Approaches to Evaluation in Education: The Silent Scientific Revolution.* New York: Praeger, 1988.

Halpern, D. F. "Student Outcomes Assessment: Introduction and Overview." In P. T. Ewell (ed.), *Assessing Educational Outcomes.* New Directions for Institutional Research, no. 47. San Francisco: Jossey-Bass, 1985.

Keiler, M. L. *The Art in Teaching Art.* Lincoln, Nebr.: University of Nebraska Press, 1961.

Mentkowski, M., and Loacker, G. "Assessing and Validating the Outcomes of College." In P. T. Ewell (ed.), *Assessing Educational Outcomes.* New Directions for Institutional Research, no. 47. San Francisco: Jossey-Bass, 1985.

National Association of Schools of Music (NASM). *The Assessment of Graduate Programs in Music.* Reston, Va.: NASM, 1985.

Nielsen, E. B. *Dance Auditions.* Princeton, N.J.: Princeton Book Company, 1984.

"Outcomes Assessment and Arts Programs in Higher Education." Briefing paper, Council of Arts Accrediting Associations, Reston, Virginia, April 1990.

Steele, J. "Evaluation College Programs Using Measures of Student Achievement and Growth." *Educational Evaluation and Policy Analysis,* 1989, 2, 357–375.

"Study-in-Depth Is a Major Concern." *AAC Liberal Education,* Summer 1990, p. 6.

Whybrew, W. E. *Measurement and Evaluation in Music.* Dubuque, Iowa: William C. Brown, 1962.

Zemsky, R. *Structure and Coherence: Measuring the Undergraduate Curriculum.* Washington, D.C.: Association of American Colleges, 1989.

Mary Anne Bunda is director of the Office of University Assessment and professor of educational leadership at Western Michigan University, Kalamazoo.

The authors emphasize graduate student socialization as a process rather than an outcome.

A Program of Institutional Research on Graduate Education

Karen Seashore Louis, Caroline Sotello Viernes Turner

Institutional Research and the Qualitative Connection

In "The Art and Science of Institutional Research," Fincher (1985) states that the purpose of institutional research was initially articulated by the American Council on Education Office of Statistical Information and Research. Thus, since its beginnings, quantitative methods have dominated institutional research efforts to meet demands for uniformly reported numerical data. While these data are important to informed decision making, Fincher (1985, p. 26) states that in too many instances institutional researchers are seen as "facts and figures people contributing neither substance nor style to institutional policy-making." Moreover, policymakers at the institutional level express concerns regarding the relevance of national or regional norms for their specific organizations.

Fincher (1985, p. 19) also quotes Henry Dyer, who concluded that institutional research needed to deal with "the real problems of particular institutions and endeavor to fit these problems into some sort of evolving generalizations." Dyer believes that institutional research can make an essential contribution by creating "a climate wherein the study of colleges and universities as societal and cultural institutions would be worthy of its own theoretical bases, methods of inquiry, and empirical findings" (p. 34). In

Our names are listed alphabetically, but we contributed equally to this chapter. We are grateful to Judith Thompson, our research assistant on the Minority Women Doctoral Students project, and to students in our qualitative research class, who conducted interviews for the departmental case studies.

his view, institutional research could become an organized search for concepts and principles that are commonly shared by members of a research specialty or profession.

We are advocates of Dyer's perspective. The examination of phenomena related to educational policy and practice as well as the extension of disciplinary knowledge base are goals of our research at the University of Minnesota. We are firmly committed to the belief that "atheoretical" institutional and evaluation research is generally less useful to the development of programs and policies than research that is grounded in more general, disciplinary frameworks. In addition, for institutional research to attract the attention of faculty in the social sciences and professional schools, it must encourage the application of disciplinary frameworks so that the data are both useful and publishable.

We also believe that qualitative case study methodology is appropriate for the study of problems within an institutional context. The qualitative case study is particularly useful in the early stages of organizational theory development, deriving strength from "its sensitivity to individual situations, patterns of relationships, contexts, and natural environments in organizations" (Hearn and Corcoran, 1988, p. 640). Although our work involves distinct studies that are carried out for different purposes, we are making every effort to embed them in a theoretical framework that is derived from sociological literature on socialization processes.

Merriam (1988) states that a qualitative case study design can provide investigators with an in-depth understanding of a problematic situation and its meaning for those involved. She points out that "the interest is in process rather than outcomes, in context rather than a specific variable, in discovery rather than confirmation. Such insights into aspects of educational practice can have a direct influence on policy, practice, and future research" (1988, p. xxi). She goes on to state that the case study approach is often the best methodology for addressing problems in which understanding is expected to lead to improved practice. It is problem-centered and situation-specific.

Let us illustrate the impact of different methodologies on the policy implications derived from institutional research. Separate, parallel investigations of the same set of institutional programs at the University of Minnesota were involved using both a close-ended survey and open-ended interviews. A close-ended survey conducted by an externally contracted firm had pointed to problems with coordination among different programs that provide services to minority students. These problems included the existence of substantial duplication of services and the need for centralized reporting and student tracking to develop a data base of information pertinent to recruitment, retention, and funding of minority students. Open-ended interviews, conducted by one of us (Turner) for another institutional research study, however, allowed minority faculty, staff, and students to provide their perspectives on minority student programs. These interviews identified serious morale issues (burnout and bitterness) among program staff and produced evidence that the existing student centers alleviate the minority student sense of cultural isolation on a predominantly white campus. Many students and staff mentioned a "welcoming cultural environment" as directly related to feelings of comfort with the campus environment. As one student respondent said, "Each of the four [ethnic/racial] groups have distinct cultures. For [minority] students, it is important to have a university [ethnic] community—a place where they can come, get a smile, and see their friends. Where they can get admissions, financial aid, and academic advising. Seeing another [ethnic] face is real important—making that connection. This is something taken for granted by the white majority."

Success in finding a level of comfort within the large undergraduate population, then, affects student retention. Thus, while services may in fact be similar and duplicative, the qualitative data suggest that the processes and context for service delivery add to the quality of university life for minority students. While the closed-ended survey identified real and pressing administrative problems, responses to open-ended questions provided further insight into the complexities of previously identified issues. Moreover, these responses have implications that contradict the survey-based recommendations to combine the separate ethnic programs and eliminate duplication of services.

A Focus on Graduate Education

There is a rich tradition of research on the effects of the college experience on the undergraduate student (Feldman and Newcomb, 1969; Astin, 1977; Fleming, 1984), but the experience of graduate students in higher education has been largely ignored. The few recent studies center around the experiences of medical students (for example, Baird, forthcoming).

It is common to view the process by which students develop and change as adult socialization. Socialization is usually defined as a process by which a person learns the ways of a group or society in order to become a functioning participant. In essence, graduate education is an interactive process in which students learn the necessary attributes and behaviors expected of an identified professional group in order to participate effectively and provide continuity to the group. Doctoral programs involve a rather lengthy period of socialization in which the individual acquires both cognitive skills and social values that are specific to the field or profession, as well as general academic values regarding research and scholarship.

In the studies described in this chapter, we examine the process of personal and professional development in graduate school using semistructured student interviews. This line of institutional research is designed to explore the experiences of doctoral students as they progress through their academic programs and to identify factors that influence the socialization process in graduate education—particularly those factors that can be affected by institutional policies. Qualitative research, and, in particular, data collection through the use of interviews, is an appropriate vehicle to assess the socialization process of graduate students. Merriam (1988, p. 3) makes the following remarks on the usefulness of this data collection technique: "[Qualitative] research focused on discovery, insight, and understanding from the perspectives of those being studied offers the greatest promise of making significant contributions to the knowledge base and practice of education. . . . Naturalistic inquiry, which focuses on meaning in context, requires a data collection instrument sensitive to underlying meaning when gathering and interpreting data. Humans are best suited for this task—and best when using methods that make use of human sensibilities such as interviewing, observing, and analyzing."

Peglow-Hoch and Walleri (1990) provide further support for the use of interviews in institutional research. They make the following observation: "The interview process allows researchers to link the individual program participants' subjective 'meanings' to objective facts" (1990, p. 6). It is assumed that students, in their own words, can identify variables that make a difference. Study results benefit the institution by pointing to positive experiences, which can be reinforced, and by illuminating negative experiences, whereby the institution can take corrective action. Such data can provide guidance to institutional leaders trying to determine what programmatic or policy changes to undertake when addressing a problem at the institutional level.

An Emerging Theoretical Framework. Our theoretical framework focuses on the *structure* of the graduate program and the *culture* of the department, as well as on students' *personal characteristics*.

Structure. Socialization to the academic community involves (1) a high-anxiety state that motivates the graduate student to learn the task and social requirements of the discipline as quickly as possible (Malaney, 1988, p. 426), (2) a learning process that is highly dependent on the behavioral and attitudinal clues provided by significant role models (professors, postdoctoral students, or more advanced graduate students), (3) role models (professors) who have a vested interest in maintaining high standards during the socialization process, as the quality of the Ph.D.'s graduated from the program will affect their own and their institution's prestige within the disciplinary community, and (4) a variety of status passages, each of which involves new learning situations and adjustments (Van Maanen and Schein, 1979, pp. 214-215).

Van Maanen and Schein (1979) identified a number of structural dimensions along which socialization may vary, four of which are particularly germane to graduate programs. While all doctoral programs have elements at both ends of each continuum, there is variation between disciplines and departments on the following:

1. *Collective versus individual emphasis,* or the degree to which critical socialization experiences occur in group settings as opposed to being tailored to the needs and concerns of the student. This dimension is particularly important as it affects the degree to which graduate students learn from their peers in their cohort (or more advanced graduate students) as well as from professors.

2. *Formal versus informal emphasis,* or the degree to which graduate student work is separate from the day-to-day work of the full-fledged scientist. In departments where graduate students have many opportunities to do "real work" alongside faculty members or even on their own, their experiences and learning are less well controlled by the department, but the situation is likely to produce more robust learning experiences.

3. *Sequential versus random steps,* or the degree to which the socialization experiences must occur in a particular order that is unambiguous and clearly communicated. Van Maanen and Schein (1979, p. 243) hypothesize that sequential socialization reduces innovativeness and adaptiveness to new situations and settings and increases conformity. For example, in a social science and a humanities department being studied at the University of Minnesota, students can obtain research assistantships at any stage in their doctoral studies. In two hard-science departments, however, it is an informal policy that graduate students do not get research assistantships until they have passed their preliminary examinations, at which point they compete with each other for the most desirable positions.

4. *Fixed versus variable timetables,* or the degree to which there is a standard for the minimum and maximum time for each stage in the graduate student's career. For example, in some programs a student expects to move through the first two years as part of a cohort and to take the preliminary examinations at roughly the same time that the other students take them. In other programs the preliminary examinations are scheduled when the adviser thinks that the student is ready. Variable socialization processes increase the graduate student's anxiety and the control of their advisers and other professors.

These dimensions are important with regard to student learning of the values and norms of the profession. For example, a department that emphasizes individualized, informal, random, and variable socialization processes provides the graduate student with an experience of intense socialization that is much more likely to have a profound impact on the student. However, it is also more difficult under these circumstances to control what the student experiences, and therefore the conformity of the student's values to professional and scholarly norms. If, for example, the student's role model is deviant from these norms in some regard, the student will have difficulty assessing this deviance because of lack of experience, or he or she may be too dependent on the role model to make judgments.

Culture. The literature also suggests that the *culture* of a department may be equally important in determining how students learn scientific values and norms. One important aspect of departmental culture is reflected in the organization of subgroups among the graduate students and faculty. For example, we hypothesized that some physical sciences are organized as *clans* (Ouichi, 1980) in which students cluster within the large laboratories of individual faculty members, and that students and faculty interact primarily within those groupings. In one department at the University of Minnesota, for example, students referred to their adviser as "father," and to the other students in the lab as "brothers." Other departments organize more along the lines of a *market* in which students must compete with each other throughout their graduate careers for the attentions and research assistantships doled out by individual, principal investigators. Van Maanen and Schein (1979) discuss the difference between *investiture versus divestiture cultures,* or the degree to which the student either is affirmed as being good "just the way you are" or, conversely, stripped of certain personal characteristics and denied individuality. Graduate programs, for example, vary widely in the degree to which faculty expect students to forgo family and social life to "live in the lab" or to do professors' work rather than work on topics of their own choosing, and so on. Divestiture processes are most likely to result in a highly committed new identity that conforms most strictly to the norms of the profession.

Student experiences will also be affected by faculty culture. For example, Louis, Blumenthal, Gluck, and Stoto (1989) showed that life sciences departments vary considerably in the degree to which they emphasize different entrepreneurial activities, such as "grantsmanship," consulting, or the development of cooperative research relationships with industry. By their own examples, faculty expose graduate students to values governing these behaviors (Victor and Cullen, 1988).

Personal Characteristics: Gender and Race. There is a considerable body of literature dealing with individual characteristics that predict successful completion of graduate school programs (Malaney, 1988), but most studies focus on the issue of predicting success. Although there are numerous studies that incorporate gender as a variable, most look at gender differences in matriculation rather than at the impact of gender on socialization experiences. Studies (mid-1970s and later) that have looked at these experiences find a variety of differences, ranging from the finding that women are more likely to receive teaching assistantships while men receive research assistantships, to the finding that women are less likely to make significant career progress than are men in the same field. These differences are documented, although at least one study suggests that there are no significant gender differences in aptitude, achievement, or other demographic characteristics within specific fields (Wertheim, Widom, and Wortzel, 1978). For the variable of race, as Malaney (1988) points out, there are few studies that have examined racial differences, and most of these focus on predictors of successful completion of degrees.

Individual Studies. The program of research that we have been developing over the past three years was unplanned but grew as our initially independent studies and separate interests were merged. In co-teaching a course in qualitative research methods to a group of students in the Higher Education Administration doctoral program, the programmatic focus of our research took shape as we used the topic of graduate education as a vehicle for our students to organize their exercises. Three main research efforts emerged.

The first effort, funded by the Center for Urban and Regional Affairs at the University of Minnesota, studied the factors leading to the successful transfer of minority students from two-year to four-year colleges. Interviews with staff members of the university's support centers for minority students raised many issues related to their own graduate careers, although this was not an initial focus of the inquiry.

The second effort involved case studies of specific graduate programs at the University of Minnesota. These were initially intended as pilot work for the development of questionnaires in a national study being conducted under funding from the National Science Foundation. However, as graduate students in the higher education program became involved, and as institution-specific issues emerged, we became committed to extending the range of departments in the investigation. To date, six departments have been studied, each involving interviews with eighteen or twenty randomly selected doctoral candidates and a semistandardized interview protocol.

The third project, which is still underway, is funded by the University of Minnesota Commission on Women through a special grant. The project involves sampling and interviewing minority women doctoral students to identify special issues that characterize their experiences. Although they are a tiny fraction of the graduate student population at the university, the commission assumes that they will have special roles to play as professional leaders, faculty members, and role models for undergraduates. The objective of the study is to sensitize both faculty and the administration to the needs of this group. The project will involve interviews with twenty randomly selected minority women enrolled in doctoral programs, and fifteen randomly selected white women.

Select Findings from the Studies

In the following sections, we briefly present findings from the three studies.

Center for Urban and Regional Affairs Study. Interviews with minority staff members who held key, student personnel positions in one of the three postsecondary institutions participating in the study, and who were also enrolled in graduate programs, revealed a central issue, which we have called "the price of talent." While these institutions provided employment to graduate students (several of whom were recruited to their positions after entering a doctoral or master's program), respondents reported taking lengthy breaks from their graduate degree programs in order to serve the higher education system. All of the student staff interviewed provided direct service to minority undergraduates and were recruited because of their minority status.

The institutions used the skills of the students but did not seem to provide incentives to move these talented individuals along in their educational programs. One American Indian employee, now working on his M.A. at another university, remarked, "I worked in [student personnel] administration at the [university] for four years. They counted my degree and work experience as a master's equivalent for salary placement so there was little incentive to go to school. Now, I am topped out [in present staff position classification]. I peaked six years ago." Another administrator identified herself as a master's-level graduate student who has been "inactive" for several years. She made the following remarks in response to a question about why minority staff continue in jobs such as hers: "I think we [minority staff] are borderline abusing ourselves. We continue undergoing this stress because we are committed to the education of students of color. We are overused."

Four other minority staff working in student personnel also described coming to a university graduate program and then finding employment in student personnel work. Each of these individuals was implementing programs to promote minority access to higher education. However, in pursuit of employment goals, they were delaying their own academic work, a situation that often filled them with bitterness and resentment. While one student staff member, who finally completed her degree in one institution and is now employed in another postsecondary institution, argued for the value of getting to know the university culture through her job, she also indicated that she would have been able to serve her community sooner if she had not taken the position.

These are students who initially came to a four-year university for educational purposes, not individuals who came for jobs. In each case, the students were the first in their families to go on to higher education, and they needed financial assistance. Employment allowed them to support themselves but did not allow timely progress toward graduate degrees. Additionally, promotional opportunities arising from these student personnel positions were limited, particularly for those not having a master's or a doctoral degree.

Implications for Policy. In these cases, the price of talent was costly for the individuals and the organizations involved. There is much talk in higher education institutions about an inability to find qualified minorities for top-level administrative and faculty positions. Could it be that the pipeline is not empty, that it is in fact full of talented individuals who, for reasons of individual economic need and the immediate personnel needs of the organization, are not completing degrees that would permit them to enter high-level administrative ranks? Qualitative data suggest that this is the case. These data also illuminated problems of low morale and burnout among several individuals interviewed. These problems appeared to adversely affect their long-term work performance and their motivation to complete higher-level degrees credentialing them to continue on their career ladders.

Implications for Theory. Quantitative data, such as the number of degrees completed, show that few minorities earn master's and doctoral degrees. While this information is useful to know, qualitative data provide an opportunity for an in-depth exploration of individual and organizational barriers to degree completion. While surveys may yield information on barriers such as money and family obligations, other factors, such as "the price of talent," interfering with graduate program progress are more readily discovered through qualitative data collection. Interviews resulted in students identifying variables that made a difference in their educational progress.

Departmental Studies. As noted earlier, six departmental doctoral programs have been studied to date, including two hard sciences, two social sciences, one humanities, and one professional program. About twenty students from each department participated in audiotaped, semi-structured interviews for a minimum of one hour. Respondents were randomly selected from a list, provided by the department, of students enrolled in the program for at least a year. They agreed to participate in the study. No monetary incentive was offered.

As shown by our framework, we anticipated significant differences in graduate student experiences across these departments, based on variations in departmental structure and culture. This expectation was confirmed. The two hard science departments were somewhat similar in structure, with each involving a program design that was collective, sequential, and fixed (students entered as a cohort, took the same courses, and were evaluated at one or several fixed points). In both departments, teaching assistantships initially supported all students, and those students who passed initial evaluation points were assigned research assistantships based on the faculty's assessment of their potential. Student socialization was quite formal in the early phases, with little personal interaction between students and professors, and informal afterward. The culture of both departments was clanlike—students socialized primarily with other students in their laboratory—and the students' career paths and progress depended to a large extent on the faculty member to whose laboratory they were assigned. Students could easily, therefore, assess where they were in the initial phases of their programs; while in their programs virtually all had opportunities to co-author papers and to present papers at professional conferences.

Throughout the process the students were very dependent on their faculty advisers. While this could be a very supportive relationship, it also was characterized in some cases by exploitation (students being asked to work all night on grants, or to do other faculty work; delays in completing dissertations because of the faculty members' research agendas) and in other cases by rebellious behaviors (reports of students yelling at faculty members when they got frustrated, or other instances of "acting out"). In sum, there was evidence (particularly in one department) of personal stress as a consequence of the dependency relationships. In addition, in one of these departments, the "entrepreneurial culture" of grant writing more than a few times resulted in exploitation of students. For example, in one department it was "known" that working with an untenured faculty member was usually more stressful, since the faculty member was also dependent on the work of his or her students to produce the research and proposals that would result in tenure.

In sharp contrast, one of the social science departments and the one humanities department in the sample had programs structured to be highly individual, random, and variable. Students did not have a clear "program" for their coursework, and there were few required courses. There was no real cohort, and the development of a sense of collectivity was also impeded by the broad age distribution among the students. Student groups were somewhat gender-segregated in one of the departments, and in another they were dominated by a student organization composed largely of the younger students who were unmarried. In neither department was support for students a standard expectation of admission; in both there were concerns about the assignment of teaching assistantships (more common) and especially research assistantships: "It's who you know" or "it's who your adviser is" were common refrains. Students moved slowly through the programs, on an uncertain timetable. In one department it was common to find students who had been in the program for ten years; in the other it was rare to find students completing their degrees in less than six years. In general, students had distant relationships with professors, whom they viewed as "busy" or "inaccessible" or "too caught up in their research." Students often differentiated themselves from the professors rather than desiring to emulate them, pointing in particular to their own preferences for teaching rather than research.

The remaining two departments differed from the previous two in both structure and culture. The programs of both the professional school department and the social science department were largely individualized (aside from a few core courses), formal (few students, even those with research assistantships, reported the strong dependency relations with mentors that occurred in the hard sciences departments), and, despite the individualized programs, quite fixed and sequential, as compared to the other social science and the humanities departments. Perhaps the clearest difference between these two groups of departments was the degree to which they were perceived as *investing* rather than *divesting*. Students in the professional school and the second social science programs had, almost uniformly, a high sense of efficacy, and the belief that their success in graduate work was dependent on their own skills and efforts.

Implications for Policy. The main institutional audiences for these studies were the departments themselves. We hoped that the studies would provide departments with information that would help them improve the quality of life for graduate students, even though the studies were not evaluations and there were no formal recommendations for change. We therefore made the reports available to the departments. At least two of them—one social science and one hard science—were sufficiently disturbed by aspects of the departments' culture and structure, as experienced by their students, to make active efforts to address areas of concern. Another department initiated a self-study modeled on the procedures used in our research and is considering changes in both curriculum and program design in response.

Implications for Theory. The studies confirmed the importance of Van Maanen and Schein's (1979) structural dimensions to understanding the experiences of doctoral students in a major research university, indicating in particular that anxiety, anger, and other socialization problems tend to be highest in departments whose doctoral programs are individualized, random, formal, and variable. However, the programs that were fixed, collective, sequential, and informal were characterized by high levels of dependency of graduate students on their advisers, which, in some circumstances and with some professors, were debilitating. Overall, we conclude from the departmental studies that program structure has as great an impact on student experiences as is exerted by the general climate of the department.

One unanticipated finding concerned the impact of student funding on culture: In the departments where all students were fully funded, and the procedures for allocating research and teaching assistantships were well understood, the students saw themselves as part of a classless meritocracy. Students who had better assignments, or who were favored by faculty, were acknowledged as "stars." In departments where not all students were funded, or in which the allocation of research and teaching assistantships was not a clear or well-understood process, there were more cliques and complaints about inequity due to gender, methodological preferences, age, and so on.

Study of Minority Women Doctoral Students. Our study of the socialization of minority women graduate students began with several objective facts for which we sought subjective or case study meanings. First, the American Council on Education (1989-1990) reports 32,943 doctorates earned nationwide in 1984-1985. Minority females earned 3.6 percent, or 1,198, of these degrees. Second, the doctorate is an access ticket for employment in college faculty positions, particularly at major research institutions. So, based on these data, the number of available minority women for such positions is limited. Third, our data on enrollment and degrees completed for doctoral-level minority women students at the University of Minnesota reflect the small numbers reported nationally.

These three facts provide national and institutional context for minority women doctoral students. However, we were still left with the question of what the data tell us about the lives of the students and the organizations involved. To begin to answer this question, we plan to interview a random sample of minority women doctoral students, and an equal number of white women doctoral students, at the University of Minnesota. By systematically examining their positive and negative experiences, our aim is to identify issues and concerns of particular importance to them. In addition to contributing to socialization theory, data from this project could be useful in developing college recruitment and retention policies and programs targeted toward making the environment as attractive and supportive as possible for minority students. We have not yet completed this study, and data analysis is, therefore, still preliminary. (The analysis eventually will compare minority and white student interviews and will use institutional data on retention, time to complete degree, and so on.) Nevertheless, a number of critical findings from the minority student interviews shed light on both theoretical and practical issues.

First, despite the strong concerns expressed by administrators about the need to recruit solid minority candidates into graduate programs, only one of the students in our sample was actively recruited by her department. In one case an adviser, whose doctoral degree is from the University of Minnesota, urged a student to apply (a form of secondary recruiting). A few students in the sample selected the University of Minnesota because they already lived in the area. In most cases, however, the minority women reported that they had conducted research about the top institutions in their fields and had actively chosen (and moved to) Minnesota. All received financial support, but only a few (in the hard sciences) had the research assistant positions that lead to close mentoring relationships with a faculty member. They reported getting along reasonably well with faculty but, with only a few exceptions, did not have special mentors.

Second, all except a few of the women are unmarried and without children, and they expressed little of the ambivalence about gender role strain that has been noted in other studies. Several commented that they could not imagine "becoming tied down" until after their educational and career goals were better established. More surprising, however, were their assertions of autonomy—and isolation. Most believed that while their families did not oppose their decisions to pursue a doctorate, the families were perplexed and "just didn't understand." Although the students reported that they had friendly relationships with other doctoral students in their programs, they did not typically have close friends on campus, and few lived on or very near the campus. When asked further about support, many reported that they had chosen to live in ethnic communities, and they achieved a sense of balance in their lives by being part of a broader community (although there was no evidence of community activism).

Third, when they discussed discrimination, virtually all of the respondents indicated that they had not experienced racial problems in their programs, or at the university in general. (They did, however, report many instances of discrimination in the larger Minneapolis community.) They were, on the other hand, vociferous and almost unanimous in reporting passive sexual bias in their programs—a sense of being passed over for less able male students. This sense was true for students in humanities, sciences, and social sciences. Only two students reported active sexual prejudice ("put-downs" in class), and in both cases the same department was involved.

Finally, one of the clearest characteristics that the minority women doctoral candidates had in common was their very high level of self-confidence. We saw little evidence of high levels of anxiety, which we expected to find; the women saw themselves as having already demonstrated their academic ability, and as being on track to successful professional careers.

Implications for Policy. A number of university policy issues arise from these findings. First, despite the official university policy of active recruitment of minority students, we found little evidence of active searching for minority women doctoral candidates. Second, although the university funds a variety of special offices and programs to serve the needs of minority students, this assistance is apparently not directed toward the social needs of these women, many of whom are often the only minority woman in their departments. Most women said that they would like opportunities to meet others like themselves. Third, the minority women reported few mentoring experiences, which may present them with problems in creating or accessing networks as they move into their active professional careers. Finally, except for the above, we suspect that minority women doctoral students have few special, unmet needs that are distinguishable from those of women doctoral students in general. One policy implication is that any genuine institutional commitment to nurture minority women in advanced degree programs should be directed to those who are at the early stages in their studies.

Implications for Theory. Our theoretical framework suggests that variables of institutional structure and culture have a potent effect on the graduate student. We were surprised to find that for our sample of minority women doctoral students, the impacts of discipline and department were less pronounced than we had expected from our departmental studies. Instead, we found that the experiences of the minority women were quite similar. We hypothesize that this finding may be, in part, due to the fact that all of these students were fully funded, but few were in close mentoring relationships. However, we also believe that the study reveals the importance of individual, personal variables that were not the main focus of our earlier studies. All of the minority women were, relative to the other students interviewed, self-confident and self-directed. While most undergraduate minority students may be anxious about success, the graduate minority students viewed themselves as successful already—and in fact they were successful, simply by being part of such a small number of enrollees.

Conclusion

Qualitative approaches have not been widely used in institutional research. We argue that such approaches can be beneficial for institutional practice as well as for disciplinary theory building. Our work suggests that qualitative research can illuminate institutional policy issues in graduate education and can also help to develop and add to theories on graduate student socialization.

Our research also indicates that qualitative case studies are particularly critical for examining student experiences, whether undergraduate or graduate, where contextual factors, whether pertaining to two-year or four-year colleges, are important. However, since our work examines students at the graduate level, observations made in this chapter focus on the use of qualitative techniques to study graduate student socialization within the context of a graduate research institution.

Graduate students undertake a narrow and specialized course of study within a department, whereas undergraduates typically take courses that introduce them to wider disciplinary fields and are encouraged for general education purposes to take courses outside of their majors. Generally, the graduate education experience is more embedded in a departmental context than is the undergraduate student experience. Loewenberg (1983) notes other characteristics that make the graduate student experience more all-consuming when compared with the undergraduate student experience. He states that "most graduate students are older" and that "their relationship to a single professor is more sustained and intimate," involving a dependence for "both immediate and long-range rewards" (1983, p. 49). The impact of departmental culture on their experiences is therefore profound, and sample surveys of students across departments, where the data are aggregated, may therefore be invalid.

Yin (1984) states that the qualitative research strategy is advantageous in situations where it is impossible to separate a phenomenon's variables from their context; and according to Merriam (1988, p. 17), a qualitative approach is most suitable when studying "a highly subjective phenomenon in need of interpreting rather than measuring. . . . Research is exploratory, inductive, and emphasizes processes rather than ends. . . . One does not manipulate variables or administer a treatment. What one does do is observe, intuit, sense what is occurring in natural setting." Our studies focus on unique departmental settings whose characteristics were not well understood ahead of time. We wanted information on how specific program structures and characteristics affect graduate student experiences. Our findings demonstrate that departments vary enormously in climate and in structure.

Finally, our studies suggest that qualitative case study approaches are particularly useful in examining minority student experiences, where cultural differences and small numbers make the advantage of survey research less clear. In considering current demographic changes in the higher education environment, Peglow-Hoch and Walleri (1990) emphasize the importance of various approaches to the task of providing institutions with "ways of knowing." They conclude that "as institutions struggle to meet the demands and needs and multifaceted communities and populations, the data obtained from quantitative research, combined with the insights gleaned from qualitative inquiry, provide educational planners with a comprehensive approach to problem solving and decision making" (1990, p. 7).

In summary, our emphasis on the study of graduate student socialization as a process rather than an outcome continues to guide our inquiries. In our view, the qualitative approach provides the most relevant data. However, we believe in the benefit of conducting institutional research with both quantitative and qualitative methods. In fact, quantitative data complement qualitative data in each of the studies reported here. In the Center for Urban and Regional Affairs study, data on minority postsecondary enrollments, transfers, and degrees granted were used to provide a state-level context for a qualitative study of the experiences of minority students, primarily undergraduates, enrolled at predominantly white two- and four-year colleges. As a result of the departmental studies, a survey examining departmental cultures is now being conducted. Finally, in addition to data collected from qualitative interviews of minority women doctoral students, we are looking at quantitative institutional data to compare the progress of minority women doctoral students with that of minority males and majority males and females. The combined results of both research strategies will provide a more complete picture of graduate education for educational policymakers and practitioners, particularly when they are trying to examine the experiences of a diverse student body within various departmental contexts.

References

American Council on Education. *1989–90 Fact Book on Higher Education.* New York: American Council on Education/Macmillan, 1989–1990.

Astin, A. W. *Four Critical Years: Effects of College on Beliefs, Attitudes, and Knowledge.* San Francisco: Jossey-Bass, 1977.

Baird, L. L. "The Melancholy of Anatomy: The Personal and Professional Development of Graduate and Professional School Students." In J. A. Smart (ed.), *Higher Education: Handbook of Theory and Research.* Vol. 6. New York: Agathon Press, in press.

Feldman, K. A., and Newcomb, T. M. *The Impact of College on Students.* Vol. 1: *An Analysis of Four Decades of Research.* San Francisco: Jossey-Bass, 1969.

Fincher, C. "The Art and Science of Institutional Research." In M. W. Peterson and M. Corcoran (eds.), *Institutional Research in Transition.* New Directions for Institutional Research, no. 46. San Francisco: Jossey-Bass, 1985.

Fleming, J. *Blacks in College: A Comparative Study of Students' Success in Black and in White Institutions.* San Francisco: Jossey-Bass, 1984.

Hearn, J. C., and Corcoran, M. E. "An Exploration of Factors Behind the Proliferation of the Institutional Research Enterprise." *Journal of Higher Education,* 1988, *59,* 634-651.

Loewenberg, P. *Decoding the Past: The Psychohistorical Approach.* New York: Knopf, 1983.

Louis, K. S., Blumenthal, D., Gluck, M., and Stoto, M. "Entrepreneurs in Academe: An Exploration of Behaviors Among Life Scientists." *Administrative Science Quarterly,* 1989, *34,* 110-131.

Malaney, G. "Graduate Education as an Area of Research in the Field of Higher Education." In J. A. Smart (ed.), *Higher Education: Handbook of Theory and Research.* Vol. 4. New York: Agathon Press, 1988.

Merriam, S. B. *Case Study Research in Education: A Qualitative Approach.* San Francisco: Jossey-Bass, 1988.

Ouichi, W. "Markets, Bureaucracies, and Class." *Administrative Science Quarterly,* 1980, *25,* 129-141.

Peglow-Hoch, M., and Walleri, R. D. "Case Studies as a Supplement to Quantitative Research: Evaluation of an Intervention Program for High-Risk Students." *Association for Institutional Research Professional File,* 1990, *35,* 1-8.

Van Maanen, J., and Schein, E. "Toward a Theory of Organizational Socialization." In B. Staw (ed.), *Research in Organizational Behavior.* Vol. 1. Greenwich, Conn.: JAI Press, 1979.

Victor, B., and Cullen, J. B. "The Organizational Bases of Ethical Work Climates." *Administrative Science Quarterly,* 1988, *33,* 101-125.

Wertheim, E. G., Widom, C. S., and Wortzel, L. H. "Multivariate Analysis of Male and Female Professional Career Choice Correlates." *Journal of Applied Psychology,* 1978, *63,* 234-242.

Yin, R. K. *Case Study Research: Design and Method.* Newbury Park, Calif.: Sage, 1984.

Karen Seashore Louis is associate professor in the Department of Educational Policy and Administration at the University of Minnesota, Minneapolis.

Caroline Sotello Viernes Turner is assistant professor in the Department of Educational Policy and Administration at the University of Minnesota, Minneapolis.

An effort to assess the quality of academic work life at a large private research university resulted in a plan to merge qualitative and quantitative measures, but the effort also uncovered political, logistical, and fiscal issues in data collection and use.

Integrating a Qualitative and Quantitative Assessment of the Quality of Academic Life: Political and Logistical Issues

Catherine Marshall, Yvonna S. Lincoln, Ann E. Austin

What common concern is shared by a provost, a faculty senate president, and a faculty bargaining-unit leader? In the 1990s each needs finely tuned methods for assessing faculty values, gripes, and dilemmas. Too often, these actors use haphazard methods such as the unsystematic gathering of opinions from cocktail chatter, or they resort to impersonal surveys designed for the "average" faculty—and few faculties enjoy being called average!

This chapter describes the context and critical issues of one university's planning to assess the quality of academic life by combining qualitative and quantitative approaches. At the initiative of the Faculty Senate of Vanderbilt University, Nashville, Tennessee, a task force pondered the philosophical, political, logistical, and methodological issues to be faced in this type of assessment. In this chapter we chronicle their process, their strategies, their compromises, and their delineation of essential elements for successful assessment. Our chronicle provides insights to decision makers who recognize the need for and face the tasks of improving communication between faculty and administration, democratizing academic life, and identifying areas of discontent.

Quality of Life Issues

Increased attention to issues pertaining to work life, productivity, and quality of product is occurring in many organizations, both academic and nonacademic. Within higher education, much discussion and research in recent years has highlighted the challenges and pressures facing the professoriate. (In particular, see Astin and Associates, in press; Austin and Gamson, 1983; Bowen and Schuster, 1986; Clark and Lewis, 1985; Clark, Corcoran, and Lewis, 1986; Schuster, Wheeler, and Associates, 1990. Additionally, several surveys and instruments are available to help colleges and universities examine themselves as academic workplaces or assess the kind of support provided for faculty professional growth; see, for example, Lovett, 1984; Austin, Rice, and Splete, in press *a*, in press *b*.) The retrenchment that affected higher education in the 1970s and 1980s, coupled with the increasing societal demands for accountability from American colleges and universities, has contributed to the erosion of some of the qualities that faculty value in the academic workplace: support for autonomy, spirit of collegiality, and flexibility of work schedules (Austin and Gamson, 1983). Based on the results of a national survey, Bowen and Schuster (1986) expressed serious concern about the condition of the American professoriate. Of particular note, they reported that conflicting expectations for faculty to excel in both teaching and research while facing heavy demands on their time contributed (along with other factors) to anxiety, stress, alienation, and a decline in morale. Other reports in the past decade have indicated a serious decline in faculty power and participation in institutional decision making. Observers of higher education as well as faculty members themselves have expressed concern about the efficacy of traditional campus governance structures (Carnegie Foundation for the Advancement of Teaching, 1982; Anderson, 1983).

Some recent indications are that the malaise characterizing the American professoriate for the past decade and a half may be lessening. For example, the faculty survey of the Carnegie Foundation for the Advancement of Teaching (1989) indicates that faculty are currently experiencing somewhat higher morale and more positive perceptions of their workplaces. Of course, faculty experiences and perceptions vary across academic sectors and institutions. Although the positive trends are encouraging, many concerns about the academic workplace continue. Additionally, some new factors affecting American higher education make attention to the quality of faculty life in colleges and universities increasingly important.

Especially significant is the impending faculty shortage, as large numbers of current faculty retire and fewer new scholars are available to take their places (Bowen and Schuster, 1986). The erosion of working conditions in academe, the modest level of salaries in comparison to other professional career areas, and the difficulties and stringent requirements associated in recent years with achieving tenure are likely, if only partial, explanations of the shrinking pool of young people interested in entering the faculty ranks. The extent of institutional attention to the quality of the academic workplace at a college or university may well be an important factor influencing potential faculty members as they decide with which institutions to affiliate.

In short, the quality of a college or university relates directly to the commitment, expertise, and vitality of its faculty. Colleges and universities that direct attention to the quality of the academic workplace and to the concerns of the faculty about the institution as a workplace are more likely to attract and hold excellent faculty.

Colleges that recognize the importance of the quality of academic life can utilize a variety of qualitative and quantitative methods to examine their situations and identify important issues. Written surveys of faculty perceptions are often used. Such surveys can provide a broad overview of faculty views insofar as the samples usually include many faculty members, but they do not reveal the uniqueness of the individual professor's experience. Individual and group interviews, faculty retreats involving small group discussions, and observations by individuals knowledgeable about academe but from outside the institution can reveal rich information about faculty work life, concerns, and perspectives. The combination of qualitative and quantitative methods often provides the most comprehensive picture of the quality of life at an institution. Regardless of which methods are used, faculty must feel that their candid expression of perceptions and concerns will not adversely affect them in either a personal or collective way and that the process is a good-faith effort to improve the quality of life at the institution.

Vanderbilt University: A Case Study

Here we present a case study of the process of planning at Vanderbilt University to assess the quality of faculty life. Data were collected by elite (or specialized knowledge holder) interviews, participant observation, and document analysis. All three of us were members of the task force assembled to develop a process for assessing faculty views at Vanderbilt. Where quotes are used, they are the words of key participants in the planning process.

Every organization has its unique history, character, and goals. Nevertheless, the higher education community as a whole can learn from the events, successes, and failures in one instance and identify appropriate, transferable lessons for use in future planning at other institutions. This particular case of Vanderbilt's planning contains such transferable lessons. The recounting of motivations and capabilities of key actors, organizational and political constraints, philosophical and methodological debates and compromises, and strategies to obtain essential supports provides those lessons.

Two coinciding events led to the combined qualitative and quantitative assessment of faculty views at Vanderbilt in 1990. First the Faculty Senate elected Paul Dokecki president, a faculty member with experience on an earlier committee that documented the failure of the university administration to grapple with senate recommendations. President Dokecki believed that qualitative methods were needed to identify patterns of beliefs and feelings inherent to quality-of-life issues. Second, the provost sent a request to the senate to cooperate with a national survey of faculty life conducted in 1990 by Alexander Astin at the University of California, Los Angeles (Astin and Associates, in press). This survey presented the opportunity for faculty members to debate and propose alternative methods for assessing academic life. Faculty leaders saw the opportunity, felt the need to revive a moribund senate, and strongly desired, in the words of one leader, "to have an ongoing communication contact, partnership between not only the administration and the faculty but also the senate and the faculty, and that's virtually nonexistent."

A related concern, articulated during Faculty Senate President Dokecki's tenure in office, was that faculty take leadership in defining the intellectual agendas of Vanderbilt. The Faculty Forum was created to develop and present to the administration a set of agreements on intellectual missions to undergird future planning. This forum was, in part, a reaction to a general sense that the administration kept exclusive rein over academic planning. One faculty leader said, "This is particularly troublesome when you have a chancellor without any visible means of academic support . . . and an administrative style that communicated unwillingness to consult senate people on the policy issues."

The Splintered Vanderbilt "Family." The history and structure of faculty governance did little to support a faculty voice in academic or management issues. According to legend, when the Faculty Senate was created, some board of trustee members protested that they were "giving away the store." The senate was the only formal body for faculty debate, yet it had no independent budget and its decisions were always "recommendations" to the chancellor. Furthermore, faculty leaders said that "a kind of plantation mentality" existed, and the "administration wants to manage and to have us faculty people leave them alone. There is just no sense that they convey to faculty leadership that there is an important resource out here in the faculty that they want to take seriously."

One faculty member spoke of the deterioration of relations between administration and faculty as creating "a hotbed of cold alienation" since the arrival of a new chancellor and provost in 1984. Although pleased with efforts to bring faculty salaries up to comparable levels with other major universities, faculty members noted the decline of the faculty voice in setting priorities. One member said, "The administration is very interested in calling us the Vanderbilt family, but acting toward us as though we were really strangers." Still, the administration's drive to place Vanderbilt on a par with the "Big Ten" universities proved to be part of the foundation supporting an innovative assessment process.

Election to the Faculty Senate would seem an honor, but, according to senators, it became "a sentence to serve," "a waste of time," and "a gentleman's club." Also, senators said, "We'd have to spend inordinate amounts of time framing our recommendations to make them palatable to the chancellor." The senate was seen as a body unto itself; although senators were elected from their schools (there are seven schools at Vanderbilt), few saw their positions as directly representing the needs and feelings of constituents.

Finally, communication channels were empty rituals. As one faculty leader said, "The chancellor thinks he's communicating when he puts an announcement in the newspaper. That's not how you communicate. There must be some sense of individual and immediate give and take."

Clearly, the stage was set for faculty cynicism toward organizational citizenship and for a widening of the chasm between the goals, needs, values, and even language of the administration and those of the faculty.

Composing the Task Force: Credibility, Expertise, and Representation. Faculty Senate President Dokecki provided the impetus for the senate to take up the assessment agenda and for the selection of task force members. Using his contacts from twenty years at Vanderbilt, Dokecki recruited eight faculty members by promoting the opportunity to plan an innovative method for identifying faculty concerns. While there was some attempt at making the membership representative of the seven schools, Dokecki emphasized the importance of getting members with expertise, political linkages, and credibility. The task force members came from sociology, philosophy, educational administration, higher education, psychology, and nursing. Three members were experts in qualitative or quantitative methodology, two specialized in the study of higher education institutions, two were long-time and highly regarded members of the faculty, with networks across campus and years of service on a range of university committees, and one was an administrator, the associate provost (who often served as a mediator between faculty and administration).

The president appointed sociologist Dan Cornfield as chair; thenceforth, the task force became known as "the Cornfield Committee." One participant described Cornfield's special qualities for leadership, saying, "He puts himself on the line a lot. . . . He gets appropriately nervous." And another said, "He's great at group analysis . . . unbelievably good. . . . I came to admire his skill, his openness, his clarity and decisiveness about where we were, what's got to be done, and [his] effectiveness in handling practical and philosophical issues." Others echoed such sentiments, speaking of their leader's youthful enthusiasm and of his experience and credibility in working with qualitative and quantitative measures.

In commenting on the committee composition, members noted the significance of the associate provost's appointment, seeing it as a sign of administrative commitment. Cornfield made special efforts to ensure good attendance at the meetings, believing part of his leadership task was to maintain commitment and shared perspectives.

Committee Debates and Strategies. The first two meetings of the Cornfield Committee allowed the emergence of critical issues. Members pondered the national survey option, political strategies necessary for convincing the administration that it needed an ongoing method for understanding faculty needs, frustration over the powerlessness of the Faculty Senate, national trends in the study of quality of life in academia, the kinds of questions that required a qualitative approach, the value (including the political value) of quantified data, and the logistics of combining qualitative and quantitative methods. A member recalled, "We had some great philosophical discussions about governance."

Cornfield formed two subcommittees. One worked on strategies for gathering quantitative data, the other worked on the rationale and logistics for gathering qualitative data.

Remarkably, the recurring debate over qualitative versus quantitative methods never surfaced on the Cornfield Committee. One member recalled that from the beginning "everyone agreed that we wanted to empower the faculty, as well as do an excellent job of information retrieval." Instead, debates in the two subcommittees and in the group as a whole focused on defining the purpose, the audience, and the desirability of a plan (such as the Astin survey) that would yield data that could be compared with those from other institutions. The task force also sought to define the role of the expert in conducting this research. The central questions of the debates were as follows: Was the target audience the faculty, the administration, or the national community of higher education administrators and scholars? Would the research gain the administration's approval if it were something *other than* a useful management tool? Would it gain faculty approval and participation if it looked like a management tool? Was this to be pure research aimed solely at documenting academic quality-of-life issues or was it to have the eventual purpose of creating an ongoing process of communication and democratization to improve Vanderbilt's quality of life?

A consensus emerged: "We talked enough about the importance of the audience, access, the cost, while realizing that the ultimate task was to get a process that would be useful at reasonable cost, the ultimate destination of which would be the administration through the senate. You only have to have administrative encouragement."

Research Purposes. Three purposes were proposed and debated. First, participation in Astin's national survey was proposed as a way to be part of the national picture and to assess Vanderbilt in comparison with other universities in a standardized survey. Administrators were willing to fund that research. But one faculty leader ridiculed the use of the Astin survey, saying, "It sort of compares us to what the norm is, that is to some sort of average. When you do that, what you're doing is assuring yourself an 'also-ran' status. . . . And we are not going to be able to deal with our faculty because our faculty's problems and dissatisfactions have very little to do with how other faculties are."

A second argument favored a methodologically precise strategy of tailoring both the qualitative and quantitative data collection to a Vanderbilt-specific context, throwing aside the urge for national comparison. This study would give a "snapshot" status report finely tuned to the Vanderbilt faculty and issues.

A third argument was that the task force should, instead, work toward the goal of creating and maintaining a mechanism for faculty members to communicate with the senate and with administration. One leader reflected, "I argued that if this is going to be effective over time, then you really ought to have it over time, to get a cumulative effect and an ongoing data set—a kind of monitoring process."

The Role of Experts. In summarizing one of the inherent tensions of the committee, a faculty member recalled that "the qualitative methodology debate especially evoked intensive discussion of professional expertise versus participatory democracy as the guiding values for structuring the methodology." Some faculty argued that expert methodologists should be recruited to collect the data; others argued that the ultimate goal was the creation of a democratic process by utilizing senate facilitators (regardless of their methodological expertise) through whom all faculty members could voice their opinions. One task force member described "a recurring tension between the people who really strongly pressed for grassroots participatory democracy versus those who pushed the role of the expert professional. . . . On the qualitative side, the issue was, who's going to run the meetings? And some wanted qualified faculty members who are trained in qualitative methods of the Marshall/Lincoln type. Others wanted to ensure getting interested faculty, regardless of their know-how in qualitative methods, to run the meetings because of their enthusiasm. . . . There was some desire to make sure the questionnaire used standard survey construction processes to pull questions from other successful surveys, emphasizing the role of the expert. Others pressed for using the qualitative findings to formulate the questionnaire."

All discussion of methodology was overridden by careful strategizing to appeal to important audiences. This political concern was used to sway members toward methodological tolerance. One task force member said, "I think whatever one guesses by way of statistical data on questionnaires is essentially backup, sort of reliability tests, which have basically a political value and not much more. And they're useful because if you say faculty are concerned about salaries, everybody says 'of course.' But if you say 78 percent of the faculty have indicated that they are strongly unhappy, you've got something that has more force."

Politics, Efficiency, and Cost-Effectiveness. A related political as well as philosophical and methodological issue was the need to make the process efficient and low-cost yet also effective. The task force committee and subcommittees talked about working within constraints. One leader recalled,

"We knew there might be some reluctance on the part of administration, so we couldn't let methodology be an excuse for them to turn it down. But on one level, faculty assessment is a search for truth, so it's motherhood and apple pie. On the other hand, if you really got in touch with the faculty pulse, that might put you on the spot about things." Another added, "We knew to present a constructive theme like integration and community building as what would fly politically . . . rather than use the militant approach or talking about the authority structure needing decentralization. We had to talk about how it's efficient and expedient to build a community. . . . Those were conscious choices of political rhetoric."

Financial constraints loomed: "We kept it cheap by using free faculty expertise for supervising the qualitative data collection and analysis and for designing the survey. It will be an act of love. But we can't do it without administration's approving the dollars."

In addition to political and financial constraints, some committee members argued that they must anticipate the reactions of the faculty audience. In the qualitative subcommittee, some feared that a stringently meticulous process would appear "ridiculous and burdensome," inviting scorn from the administration and fear from faculty, who would not get involved in a laborious and time-consuming process. The quantitative subcommittee tossed aside their arguments for cost-effectiveness through sampling as they pondered the faculty audience. They recommended a survey that contacted every individual faculty member so that all would feel represented, even though such a survey would be more costly.

Creating Credibility and Culminating Compromises. For the assessment to garner faculty and administration support, the committee realized that they needed to anticipate misgivings and resistance. Although the committee membership already had been selected to reflect both the authority and skill of experts and the credibility of the good faculty citizens, the committee still worked to maximize the credibility of their plan. Cornfield carefully managed the discussions and the work to avoid the appearance of militancy, knowing that radical rhetoric and action would scare some faculty and ensure blockage by the administration.

As the subcommittees completed their work, each presented a work plan to Cornfield, who integrated the two strands and designed a flowchart of activities. The ensuing debates centered on faculty reactions: "Administrators had better not 'use' it [against faculty, or in order to manipulate faculty]. If that's the perception by faculty, and I think that's what the provost wants, then faculty will see it as initiated by those terrible administration guys." The debates led to compromises, and, incorporating those compromises, Cornfield wrote a final draft of the report.

The qualitative strand would be supervised by faculty members with expertise in qualitative methodology. Data would be collected via a "town meeting" format, wherein each school solicited faculty sentiments and compiled them as qualitative data. A content analysis would be conducted to identify key issues and questions raised. Using the qualitative findings to generate survey items, as well as incorporating relevant items from national surveys, faculty members who were expert in survey construction would devise a questionnaire. Every faculty member would receive this questionnaire. Based on the expected use of volunteer faculty expertise and paid graduate student assistance, the cost was projected at $5,441. This plan was submitted for Faculty Senate approval in May 1990, and then for administration support and budget approval. Implementation of the plan was underway in fall 1990.

Political and Logistical Issues in Data Collection and Analysis

During committee meetings and negotiations, several issues surfaced as significant to completion of the faculty assessment effort. These issues have implications not only for quality-of-life research but also for institutional research in higher education more broadly.

Campus Politics. From its inception, the committee was aware that the faculty assessment effort would be understood differently among the diverse constituencies on campus. Over time, the Cornfield Committee attempted to balance the Faculty Senate desire for improved faculty communication, specifically on issues that the faculty felt were underdiscussed or underemphasized but critical to their working lives, and the committee's belief that at least some faculty would view the assessment effort and results as a managerial tool, to be used (or not) as the administration saw fit. Thus, the questions often raised around institutional research data surfaced in this effort: To what purposes will the data be dedicated, and who will have access to them?

Concerns about the assessment effort were voiced in a variety of ways. The Faculty Senate was consistent in its support for the creation of channels of communication among the faculty, and for the first avenue of that communication to be the faculty's own constructions of academic life at the university. Members of the committee were anxious about whether faculty could or would participate in an effort to communicate their concerns, and apprehensive about the perceived levels of disaffection and anomie in some departments and schools. At the same time, the committee was concerned about possible administrative reactions to the proposal for a faculty survey.

With strong agreement among committee members, the proposal was pushed forward, with the internal assessment dedicated, insofar as possible, to two outcomes: discovery of what the faculty see as the conditions of their academic work life and formulation of a model for long-term participatory democracy. Amidst speculation about the reactions of the provost and chancellor, the proposal was presented to the administration. Final acceptance of the proposal, and the granting of funds to support it, were viewed by members of the committee as positive, strong signs of commitment from the central administration.

Balancing and Integrating Qualitative and Quantitative Approaches. The committee was unanimously agreed that both qualitative and quantitative data should be sought. How they should be sought was a matter of fine-grained negotiation. Early on, committee members agreed that the process of assessment would be enhanced by solicitation of the emic ("insider," as opposed to "outsider") views of the faculty on the hows and whys of the assessment, on their work and organizational lives, and on the need for open communication. The question for the committee was how to balance the quest for meaning and significance (a task for qualitative research) with the power of numbers to persuade and prompt action (the quantitative response), especially in an environment where numbers play a strong role in decision making, but where meaning, symbols, rites, rituals, and myths also are potent and compelling.

A two-step process—qualitative grounding and quantitative surveys—emerged as a workable way of combining both approaches. Committee members concurred that qualitative data would provide the dense texture of the assessment, while quantitative data would provide the validity check. This agreement was negotiated with sensitivity toward the expertise of the various committee members and with pragmatism regarding what would be considered compelling data at that particular point in the university's history.

By the design of the study, qualitative data were to be gathered through "town meetings" in various departments, and, when small enough to permit face-to-face interaction, in schools. In large units such as the School of Arts and Sciences, departments would be grouped for mutual discussions by interest areas: hard sciences, social sciences, and humanities.

The process of assessment would include having such groups meet with one or more "facilitators," who would ask questions and have group members raise questions. Skilled notetakers would write descriptions of the proceedings, which would then be transcribed into more detailed field-notes. One of the committee members, an expert in content analysis, would then examine the field notes, extracting major, common themes and concerns expressed by the faculty but also looking for interests that appeared to bear on just one or a few schools.

From this content analysis of the qualitative data, a survey would then be constructed, providing a "grounded" questionnaire to be sent to all faculty in the arts and sciences and professional schools (engineering, medicine, nursing, education, business, divinity, and music). The content analyst agreed to work closely with the questionnaire constructor (also a methodological expert) to make certain that the final questionnaire reflected with fidelity and subtlety the concerns voiced by faculty during the town meetings in their respective schools or departments. Among committee members and the Faculty Senate leadership, the general feeling was that "it's an exciting possibility."

Credibility. Credibility, of both the committee members and the data, was seen as a major factor in this venture. Thus, committee members were chosen for the general respect that they enjoyed among other faculty members, for their expertise in some arena, or for a combination of these factors.

Credibility of the data was another matter. A serious issue in any study of the faculty work life is whether or not all the faculty's views have been appropriately and sufficiently represented. In this instance, the quest for representation led to the town meeting, "focus group" format.

In addition, the skills of the group facilitator and of the group "secretary" (both faculty members) in recording faculty responses are critical to the success of the research. A facilitator who is not a careful listener and a gentle discussion guide, or a recording secretary who fails to grasp the essence of faculty discussions, render the process virtually useless for purposes of analysis and remedial action. With these skills in mind, members of the Faculty Senate and the committee chairman searched for and requested the services of faculty members (often, Faculty Senate representatives) who were reputed to have good group skills and adroitness in listening accurately and sympathetically. By basing the original data collection efforts in the "local" faculty groupings, the goal was to collect not only faculty members' constructions of their lives but also constructions shared among the groupings. A strenuous effort was made to ensure representation that was both broad (in terms of participation) and thick (in terms of having the widest range of issues emerge), and to create every opportunity possible for faculty to participate. For instance, multiple meetings were planned for many "local" groups, and letters were sent individually to all faculty to invite them to the meetings and to offer them the opportunity to comment on any aspect of their work lives.

Despite the careful methodological design, the planners feared that the call for widespread faculty participation would be met with faculty indifference, fear, pursuit of other agendas, and alienation. Thus, while the qualitative data might be both compelling and inviting, apprehension regarding the extent of the response to both the "town meetings" and wider survey was, and remains, high. In spite of this apprehension, however, the committee has won approval for the process and will continue to seek faculty input.

Finances. The Faculty Senate, unlike an institutional research office, operates without funding, save those funds granted by the central administration, particularly the provost. Where and how to find the resources above and beyond volunteer work was a concern. Thus, a very modest budget was proposed, one that relied on the goodwill of faculty to volunteer their time and expertise. The Faculty Senate, upon acceptance of the committee's proposal of a process and budget for the research, requested the requisite funds from central administration. The senate's precarious power was highlighted as leaders waited five months for approval of their initiative. But approval was granted and research assistants, computer time, and other expenses were provided to begin the effort.

Implications for Institutional Research

Research on and in institutions may take several forms: institutional-level research, program review (typically, at the statewide level), reviews for accreditation purposes, and other types of self-studies. Studies of organizational life are often initiated by institutional research units, but as this case study shows, such studies can emerge from other groups or units. The case study reported here arose from a faculty governance unit's interest in and concern about faculty quality-of-life issues. The problems faced during this effort are also confronted, albeit in different forms, by most campus-based, institutional research units.

First, credibility and, more generally, political concerns are important to institutional research units, although in a different way from the effort reported here. Occasionally, institutional research units do not enjoy much credibility on their own campuses, and their offices are looked upon as siphons of scarce resources from institutional budgets. Institutional research often has to be "sold" to the faculty as a useful and worthwhile expenditure of resources, and it is sometimes difficult for faculty to see the work of such offices as critical to their own teaching and research. The invisibility of such offices, the structure that mandates reports to the central administration, and the abstraction of their data often serve to create a distance from faculty, who do not see the potential contributions of institutional research to disciplinary concerns. Since faculty rarely have occasion to communicate with institutional researchers and do not understand their contribution to a variety of management information activities necessary to the institution's operation, institutional research offices can suffer from a serious lack of credibility.

Political concerns inherent to institutional research are often serious. When faculty are asked, for instance, to buy into institutional research efforts, resistance is sometimes mounted, and faculty often raise some of the same issues that surfaced in this study: "Who are these data for?" "Will I be disadvantaged by this effort in any way?" "For what purposes will these data be used?" "Are faculty positions on the line?" The link between statewide program review efforts and institutional research in particular has been troublesome on these issues, since faculty know that program review can and has led to program discontinuation and to termination or redeployment of faculty. The certain knowledge that the information will be used for different ends by different constituencies on and off the campus leads to wariness. Even when an institutional review effort is publicly aimed at improving faculty work conditions, some suspicion is unavoidable among faculty.

The financing of institutional research studies is typically not a concern since institutional research funds are part of the college or university's overall budget. In this case study, it was a concern because a request had to be prepared for funding of the study. Still, finances are a consideration in that resources are typically never enough to do all of the work that could be done, and many interesting studies and analyses remain undone because of the need to respond to other, more pressing concerns such as budget and enrollment analyses, legislative requests, and projections for formula funding requests. Where formal budget lines do not exist, attention must be paid to the task of securing funds for studies.

With respect to the qualitative-quantitative balance achieved by the Vanderbilt committee, another interesting lesson can be extracted. Researchers in higher education understand that quantitative data do not completely meet the need for sophisticated and fine-grained postsecondary policymaking. Such data provide only one kind of information base needed to study the highly diverse contexts and policies of radically different institutions. On this point, qualitative data have strengths that compensate for the weaknesses of strictly quantitative data (Marshall, 1985). But the issue of augmenting decision- and policy-making capabilities by incorporating qualitative analyses into studies previously dominated by quantitative data has led to questions about cost, time, training of researchers to collect and analyze such data, and formats for displaying the data. Clearly, qualitative data represent a major investment in time and, therefore, cost, and many institutional researchers have no formal training in this work. For these reasons, the question that researchers most often ask themselves—"What are the best data that I can obtain at the least cost per unit?"—has led to the assumption that the best data obtainable are those least costly to collect, which tend to be quantitative.

Because the case study reported here represents a time-bound and finite project (at least its first iteration), the combination of quantitative and qualitative data was presumed to be the most holistic and the most persuasive. But in a permanent operation, qualitative data collection and analysis may prove extraordinarily costly. Thus, their use might be subtly discouraged when efficiency becomes a primary concern. Although in the wider world of higher education, discipline-based research, qualitative methods are increasingly taught and used (Chaffee and Tierney, 1988; Tierney, 1988; Lincoln, 1989), institutional research offices may not have the luxury of establishing qualitative data bases. However, it could be equally well argued that these offices cannot afford the luxury of not establishing them. Qualitative data possess high political utility for two reasons: They are accessible to persons without extensive quantitative skills or training, and they tend to be reported in natural language formats, which provide a common vocabulary for all members of the college community (Marshall, 1984).

Finally, the issue of faculty representation is important. In the present case study, representation was linked to strenuous efforts to invite the input and participation of faculty members in any manner with which they felt comfortable. But it is not always clear to faculty whether their interests are represented fully and fairly in institutional research efforts. The role of institutional research data in central administration and management and the growing faculty distrust of and distance from the central administration can lead to faculty perceptions that their concerns are not being adequately addressed. Institutional researchers must help faculty members understand how their worlds are represented, making certain that faculty issues are addressed and disseminating the results of institutional research studies more widely on campus.

The lessons from the Vanderbilt case study have applicability in several different ways to institutional research operations. Increasingly, institutional research efforts will have to be directed toward assessing the quality of faculty work life if institutions are to retain the good faculty that they have so assiduously recruited. Moreover, this task of retaining qualified and productive faculty will become increasingly difficult as faculty shortages intensify over the next twenty years (Bowen and Schuster, 1986). Also, assessments of the quality of faculty life and the workplace will be inadequate if efforts are not made to ensure that faculty views are well represented, if faculty constructions of their lives are not sought, and if faculty do not understand the processes and expected outcomes of the assessments. Equally clearly, budget constraints mandate that assessment efforts of several sorts—faculty quality-of-life studies, program reviews, accreditation studies, and student outcomes assessment—be completed in a more integrated, less piecemeal way, so that data collected for one purpose can be used economically and prudently for multiple ends and multiple audiences (Lincoln, 1990).

Postscript

This case study, and the assessment effort it represents, are still "in progress." In the process of conducting the original faculty assessment, issues arose that might be approached differently at this site in subsequent studies, or on other campuses. For example, the group meeting "facilitators" were elected senators from the academic colleges and schools, but they might be designated differently at other institutions. These individuals convened groups from their own colleges and schools, but that need not be necessary.

The facilitators were not given particular instructions regarding the number of times to schedule town meetings, the number of group members best suited to this kind of interaction, or whether or what kind of groundwork needed to be laid. Facilitators were not given formal training but were encouraged to choose as partners in this enterprise recorders who were known to be good notetakers. Thus, implementation details, such as allotment of a sufficient number of meetings to permit all faculty at least one opportunity to attend, and data quality assurances were not all worked out ahead of time.

Methodological decisions were made consonant with the climate of this particular institution, insofar as the original task force could foresee and plan. But that planning has not obviated all difficulties, and other institutions might wish to make strategic methodological decisions based on their unique contexts.

References

Anderson, R. E. *Higher Education in the 1970s: Preliminary Technical Report for Participating Institutions.* New York: Institute of Higher Education, Teachers College, Columbia University, 1983.

Astin, A., and Associates. *The American College Teacher.* Los Angeles: Higher Education Research Institute, University of California, in press.

Austin, A. E., and Gamson, Z. F. *Academic Workplace: New Demands, Heightened Tensions.* ASHE-ERIC Higher Education Research Report No. 10. Washington, D.C.: Association for the Study of Higher Education, 1983.

Austin, A. E., Rice, R. E., and Splete, A. P. *The Academic Workplace Audit.* Washington, D.C.: Council of Independent Colleges, in press a.

Austin, A. E., Rice, R. E., and Splete, A. P. *A Good Place to Work: Sourcebook for the Academic Workplace.* Washington, D.C.: Council of Independent Colleges, in press b.

Bowen, H. R., and Schuster, J. H. *American Professors: A National Resource Imperiled.* New York: Oxford University Press, 1986.

Carnegie Foundation for the Advancement of Teaching. *The Control of the Campus.* Princeton, N.J.: Princeton University Press, 1982.

Carnegie Foundation for the Advancement of Teaching. *The Condition of the Professoriate: Attitudes and Trends, 1989.* Princeton, N.J.: Princeton University Press, 1989.

Chaffee, E. E., and Tierney, W. G. *Collegiate Culture and Leadership Strategies.* New York: American Council on Education/Macmillan, 1988.

Clark, S. M., Corcoran, M., and Lewis, D. R. "The Case for an Institutional Perspective on Faculty Development." *Journal of Higher Education,* 1986, 57 (2), 176–195.

Clark, S. M., and Lewis, D. R. (eds.). *Faculty Vitality and Institutional Productivity: Critical Perspectives for Higher Education.* New York: Teachers College Press, 1985.

Lincoln, Y. S. "Trouble in the Land: The Paradigm Revolution in the Academic Disciplines." In J. A. Smart (ed.), *Higher Education: Handbook of Theory and Research.* Vol. 5. New York: Agathon Press, 1989.

Lincoln, Y. S. "Program Review, Accreditation, Processes, and Outcomes Assessment: Pressures on Institutions of Higher Education." *Evaluation Practice,* 1990, 11 (1), 13–23.

Lovett, C. M. *Vitality Without Mobility: The Faculty Opportunities Audit.* Current Issues in Higher Education No. 4. Washington, D.C.: American Association for Higher Education, 1984.

Marshall, C. "The Case Study Evaluation: A Means for Managing Organizational and Political Tensions." *Evaluation and Program Planning*, 1984, 7, 253–266.

Marshall, C. "Field Studies and Educational Administration and Policy: The Fit, the Challenge, the Benefits, the Costs." *Urban Education*, 1985, 20 (1), 61–81.

Schuster, J. H., Wheeler, D. W., and Associates. *Enhancing Faculty Careers: Strategies for Development and Renewal.* San Francisco: Jossey-Bass, 1990.

Tierney, W. G. "Organizational Culture in Higher Education: Defining the Essentials." *Journal of Higher Education*, 1988, 59 (1), 2–21.

Catherine Marshall is professor of educational leadership at the University of North Carolina, Chapel Hill.

Yvonna S. Lincoln is professor of higher education at Texas A&M University, College Station.

Ann E. Austin is associate professor in the Department of Educational Administration, Michigan State University, East Lansing.

Qualitative resource landmarks have been collected to provide an overview of the intellectual landscape.

Qualitative Resource Landmarks

David M. Fetterman

The studies presented in this collection provide only a glimpse at the vast array of qualitative concepts and techniques available for institutional research. Indeed, the collection serves primarily to introduce the variety of qualitative approaches available. Another practical guide to some of the most common qualitative evaluation approaches used today is *Qualitative Approaches to Evaluation in Education: The Silent Scientific Revolution* (Fetterman, 1988b), which provides insight into the topography of the qualitative dimension, including discussions of ethnography, naturalistic inquiry, generic pragmatic (sociological) qualitative inquiry, and connoisseurship and criticism.

Once researchers have a overview of the intellectual landscape, they can select individual approaches for further study. If ethnography is the approach of choice, *Ethnography: Step by Step* (Fetterman, 1989) is a popular fieldwork textbook; the book discusses concepts and techniques, equipment, analysis, writing, and ethics. If naturalistic inquiry is selected, *Naturalistic Inquiry* (Lincoln and Guba, 1985) is highly recommended as the standard textbook in the field for this approach. One of the most popular approaches adopted by evaluators is the generic approach, detailed in *Qualitative Evaluation Methods* (Patton, 1980) and *Qualitative Evaluation and Research Methods* (Patton, 1990). The only qualitative approach based on art rather than science is connoisseurship and criticism, which is discussed in *The Educational Imagination: On the Design and Evaluation of School Programs* (Eisner, 1985). A mild critique of each approach is presented in "The Quiet Storm" (Fetterman, 1988c).

Myriad additional resources are available for the researcher interested in a more detailed picture of various aspects of qualitative research that cross-cut specific qualitative approaches. Case studies represent the most graphic means of portraying qualitative research, and *Case Study Research* (Yin, 1989) best describes how to conduct case studies. *Designing Qualitative Research* (Marshall and Rossman, 1989) provides an invaluable guide to developing a qualitative research design. *Qualitative Data Analysis* (Miles and Huberman, 1984) provides a pragmatic set of analytic tools for both the ethnographer and the survey researcher, including a vast array of matrices. *Writing Up Qualitative Research* (Wolcott, 1990) provides an invaluable guide to the final stages of the research process: from beginning to write, to editing, to getting published.

A brief list of additional readings is provided below to shed light on both general and specific concerns in qualitative research. Some of these texts provide a basic grounding in qualitative research (or in a specific type of qualitative research), others focus on elements of an approach.

Basics of Qualitative Research: Grounded Theory Procedures and Techniques (Strauss and Corbin, 1990)
Educational Evaluation: Ethnography in Theory, Practice, and Politics (Fetterman and Pitman, 1986)
Ethnography in Educational Evaluation (Fetterman, 1984)
Excellence and Equality: A Qualitatively Different Perspective on Gifted and Talented Education (Fetterman, 1988a)
Experiencing Fieldwork: An Inside View of Qualitative Research (Shaffir and Stebins, 1991)
Focus Groups as Qualitative Research (Morgan, 1988)
Fourth-Generation Evaluation (Guba and Lincoln, 1989)
Interpretive Interactionism (Denzin, 1989)
Learning From the Field: A Guide from Experience (Whyte, 1984)
Living the Ethnographic Life (Rose, 1990)
Participant Observation (Jorgensen, 1989)
Qualitative Methodology (Van Maanen, 1983)
Speaking of Ethnography (Agar, 1986)
The Paradigm Dialog (Guba, 1990)

A variety of professional organizations also focus on qualitative research in one form or another. The task of establishing a collegial network of qualitative researchers is much like establishing a network of computer users: in addition to providing support, these groups of individuals share specific tools or insights into the problems associated with certain techniques. The following organizations are highly recommended: American Anthropological Association (Council on Anthropology and Education, National Association for the Practice of Anthropology, and other organizations), American Educational Research Association (Qualitative Special Interest Group), American Evaluation Association (Qualitative Methods Topical

Interest Group), American Psychological Association, American Sociological Association, Association for the Study of Higher Education, Ethnography and Education Forum, and Society for Applied Anthropology.

This list of resources is not meant to be definitive or exhaustive, only a good beginning. The use of qualitative approaches enhances our understanding of how institutions function as living, breathing organisms. This knowledge has already been used to facilitate the missions of a host of organizations and institutions. The utility of each qualitative approach (and technique) discussed in this collection is limited only by the researcher's imagination and creativity.

References

Agar, M. *Speaking of Ethnography*. Newbury Park, Calif.: Sage, 1986.

Denzin, N. K. *Interpretive Interactionism*. Newbury Park, Calif.: Sage, 1989.

Eisner, E. *The Educational Imagination: On the Design and Evaluation of School Programs*. New York: Macmillan, 1985.

Fetterman, D. M. *Ethnography in Educational Evaluation*. Newbury Park, Calif.: Sage, 1984.

Fetterman, D. M. *Excellence and Equality: A Qualitatively Different Perspective on Gifted and Talented Education*. Albany: State University of New York Press, 1988a.

Fetterman, D. M. (ed.). *Qualitative Approaches to Evaluation in Education: The Silent Scientific Revolution*. New York: Praeger, 1988b.

Fetterman, D. M. "The Quiet Storm." In D. M. Fetterman (ed.), *Qualitative Approaches to Evaluation in Education: The Silent Scientific Revolution*. New York: Praeger, 1988c.

Fetterman, D. M. *Ethnography: Step by Step*. Newbury Park, Calif.: Sage, 1989.

Fetterman, D. M., and Pitman, M. (eds.). *Educational Evaluation: Ethnography in Theory, Practice, and Politics*. Newbury Park, Calif.: Sage, 1986.

Guba, E. G. *The Paradigm Dialog*. Newbury Park, Calif.: Sage, 1990.

Guba, E. G., and Lincoln, Y. S. *Fourth-Generation Evaluation*. Newbury Park, Calif.: Sage, 1989.

Jorgensen, D. L. *Participant Observation*. Newbury Park, Calif.: Sage, 1989.

Lincoln, Y. S., and Guba, E. G. *Naturalistic Inquiry*. Newbury Park, Calif.: Sage, 1985.

Marshall, C., and Rossman, G. B. *Designing Qualitative Research*. Newbury Park, Calif.: Sage, 1989.

Miles, M. B., and Huberman, A. M. *Qualitative Data Analysis*. Newbury Park, Calif.: Sage, 1984.

Morgan, D. L. *Focus Groups as Qualitative Research*. Newbury Park, Calif.: Sage, 1988.

Patton, M. Q. *Qualitative Evaluation Methods*. Newbury Park, Calif.: Sage, 1980.

Patton, M. Q. *Qualitative Evaluation and Research Methods*. Newbury Park, Calif.: Sage, 1990.

Rose, D. *Living the Ethnographic Life*. Newbury Park, Calif.: Sage, 1990.

Shaffir, W. B., and Stebins, R. A. *Experiencing Fieldwork: An Inside View of Qualitative Research*. Newbury Park, Calif.: Sage, 1991.

Strauss, A., and Corbin, J. *Basics of Qualitative Research: Grounded Theory Procedures and Techniques*. Newbury Park, Calif.: Sage, 1990.

Van Maanen, J. *Qualitative Methodology*. Newbury Park, Calif.: Sage, 1983.

Whyte, W. F. *Learning from the Field: A Guide from Experience.* Newbury Park, Calif.: Sage, 1984.

Wolcott, H. *Writing Up Qualitative Research.* Newbury Park, Calif.: Sage, 1990.

Yin, R. K. *Case Study Research: Design and Method.* Newbury Park, Calif.: Sage, 1989.

David M. Fetterman is administrator and professor of education at Stanford University, Stanford, California, and Sierra Nevada College, Incline Village, Nevada. He is also president of the American Anthropological Association's Council on Anthropology and Education.

INDEX

ORDERING INFORMATION

NEW DIRECTIONS FOR INSTITUTIONAL RESEARCH is a series of paperback books that provides planners and administrators in all types of academic institutions with guidelines in such areas as resource coordination, information analysis, program evaluation, and institutional management. Books in the series are published quarterly in Fall, Winter, Spring, and Summer and are available for purchase by subscription as well as by single copy.

SUBSCRIPTIONS for 1991 cost $45.00 for individuals (a savings of 20 percent over single-copy prices) and $60.00 for institutions, agencies, and libraries. Please do not send institutional checks for personal subscriptions. Standing orders are accepted.

SINGLE COPIES cost $14.95 when payment accompanies order. (California, New Jersey, New York, and Washington, D.C., residents please include appropriate sales tax.) Billed orders will be charged postage and handling.

DISCOUNTS FOR QUANTITY ORDERS are available. Please write to the address below for information.

ALL ORDERS must include either the name of an individual or an official purchase order number. Please submit your order as follows:
  Subscriptions: specify series and year subscription is to begin
  Single copies: include individual title code (such as IR1)

MAIL ALL ORDERS TO:
  Jossey-Bass Inc., Publishers
  350 Sansome Street
  San Francisco, California 94104

FOR SALES OUTSIDE OF THE UNITED STATES CONTACT:
  Maxwell Macmillan International Publishing Group
  866 Third Avenue
  New York, New York 10022

OTHER TITLES AVAILABLE IN THE
NEW DIRECTIONS FOR INSTITUTIONAL RESEARCH SERIES
Patrick T. Terenzini, Editor-in-Chief
Ellen Earle Chaffee, Associate Editor

U.S. Postal Service

STATEMENT OF OWNERSHIP, MANAGEMENT AND CIRCULATION
Required by 39 U.S.C. 3685

1A. Title of Publication	1B. PUBLICATION NO.	2. Date of Filing
New Directions for Institutional Research	0 9 8 - 9 3 0	10/11/91

3. Frequency of Issue	3A. No. of Issues Published Annually	3B. Annual Subscription Price
Quarterly	Four (4)	$45 (individual) $60 (institutional)

4. Complete Mailing Address of Known Office of Publication *(Street, City, County, State and ZIP+4 Code) (Not printers)*
350 Sansome Street, San Francisco, Ca 94104-1310

5. Complete Mailing Address of the Headquarters of General Business Offices of the Publisher *(Not printer)*
(above address)

6. Full Names and Complete Mailing Address of Publisher, Editor, and Managing Editor *(This item MUST NOT be blank)*
Publisher *(Name and Complete Mailing Address)*
Jossey-Bass Inc., Publishers (above address)

Editor *(Name and Complete Mailing Address)*
Patrick T. Terenzini, Center for the Study of Higher Education, 133 Willard Building, The Pennsylvania State University, University Park, PA 16802

Managing Editor *(Name and Complete Mailing Address)*
Lynn Luckow, President, Jossey-Bass, Inc., Publishers (above address)

7. Owner *(If owned by a corporation, its name and address must be stated and also immediately thereunder the names and addresses of stockholders owning or holding 1 percent or more of total amount of stock. If not owned by a corporation, the names and addresses of the individual owners must be given. If owned by a partnership or other unincorporated firm, its name and address, as well as that of each individual must be given. If the publication is published by a nonprofit organization, its name and address must be stated.) (Item must be completed.)*

Full Name	Complete Mailing Address
Maxwell Communications Corp., plc	Headington Hill Hall Oxford OX30BW U.K.

8. Known Bondholders, Mortgagees, and Other Security Holders Owning or Holding 1 Percent or More of Total Amount of Bonds, Mortgages or Other Securities *(If there are none, so state)*

Full Name	Complete Mailing Address
same as above	same as above

9. For Completion by Nonprofit Organizations Authorized To Mail at Special Rates *(DMM Section 423.12 only)*
The purpose, function, and nonprofit status of this organization and the exempt status for Federal income tax purposes *(Check one)*

(1) ☐ Has Not Changed During Preceding 12 Months	(2) ☐ Has Changed During Preceding 12 Months	*(If changed, publisher must submit explanation of change with this statement.)*

10. Extent and Nature of Circulation *(See instructions on reverse side)*	Average No. Copies Each Issue During Preceding 12 Months	Actual No. Copies of Single Issue Published Nearest to Filing Date
A. Total No. Copies *(Net Press Run)*	1900	1975
B. Paid and/or Requested Circulation 1. Sales through dealers and carriers, street vendors and counter sales	60	7
2. Mail Subscription *(Paid and/or requested)*	1003	1007
C. Total Paid and/or Requested Circulation *(Sum of 10B1 and 10B2)*	1063	1014
D. Free Distribution by Mail, Carrier or Other Means Samples, Complimentary, and Other Free Copies	120	61
E. Total Distribution *(Sum of C and D)*	1183	1075
F. Copies Not Distributed 1. Office use, left over, unaccounted, spoiled after printing	717	900
2. Return from News Agents	-0-	-0-
G. TOTAL *(Sum of E, F1 and 2—should equal net press run shown in A)*	1900	1975

11. I certify that the statements made by me above are correct and complete	Signature and Title of Editor, Publisher, Business Manager, or Owner Larry Ishii Vice-President

PS Form 3526, Feb. 1989 *(See instructions on reverse)*